# *The Love of the Cross*

a progressive journey

from questioning to knowing

the love of God

by

## Cathy Scott

# Table of Contents

Love never fails.

(1 Corinthians 13:8)

# FORETHOUGHT: A Story

A family moved into their ideal home in beautiful surroundings, and the children were anxious to explore their new neighborhood on their bikes. Their dad, loving his children very much, gave them the okay to do so, saying, "Go ahead. This is your home now, so enjoy yourselves." But he added a stern warning. Wanting to protect his children, he said, "Listen carefully. You can ride anywhere in the neighborhood that you would like to go, but do not go on the highway, or something very bad will happen. Now go have fun."

The children departed and had a great time, riding their bikes up and down the neighborhood streets. Eventually they came to the highway, where they stopped and stared. On the other side was enticement: a playground offering potentially endless fun. Suddenly their side of the highway, lacking the far side's appeal, appeared bland.

The children debated about what to do. The freedom that they had been given by their dad to enjoy their lives also gave them opportunity to determine their contentment. As vehicles whizzed by, the children considered the situation. "Surely," they thought, "there is sufficient time and space between the vehicles for us to cross safely, for we are the best of riders." Then they questioned what they knew, asking, "Did Dad really say that something bad *would* happen or that it *could* happen?"

In debating their dad's wisdom, the children gave preference to temptation, making their loving father's greatest nightmare a reality. He lost his children due to their lack of faith in the fullness of his loving care for them.

The children's dad had given his life to his family, working hard to give them everything that they needed to live well. But the children had wanted more than what was good for them. They had wanted to live apart from his guidelines and not be bound to his way of life. So they had tried to cross the highway to attain greater pleasure than they thought that their dad would ever be willing to offer to them. They didn't understand that their dad already had the greatest of all pleasures in sharing his life with his family and that that was the greatest gift that he could give them. Though the children lost everything, their dad lost the most, for he was left without them to love.

When relatives and neighbors heard the news, they were shocked. In their disbelief, they wanted answers to their questions: Why did the children's father ever permit them to go outside alone? Why didn't he do more to protect them? What kind of father was he?

No one understood the depth of the father's sorrow, for no one knew the extent of his love for his children to whom he had given freedom to live. No one... Not a one. They couldn't, for they weren't the children's father. They weren't "Dad."

# *The Questioning* (The Author)

Some people are of the opinion that life is a no-win scenario, for no matter what is done or not done, life always ends in death. Nonetheless, many still attempt to delay death's arrival by pouring time and money into gym memberships, health foods, nutritional supplements and items of questionable effect. Others go for the gusto that is available in this world, trying to amass enough feel good moments to offset whatever is or is not to come. All the while, war torn villages, storm ravaged regions, drought stricken lands, famine bloated bellies and overfilled hospital wards testify to the inevitable that catches up to all: "...man is destined to die once, and after that to face judgment" (Hebrews 9:27).

Residing in each of us are questions of long standing. What is the reality of life and death? Why are we living on this planet called Earth? Why were we born, and why must we die? Why is suffering a part of life? Why can't we simply let bygones be bygones and let harmony reign? Is there purpose to existence, or is life a fluke of nature? Is there more to reality than what meets the eye, or is what we see all that we get? Does eternity exist, or does time end all?

A cursory examination of Truth (referring to God and man in relationship with one another, as differentiated from the truth of general facts) can raise many questions that, if left unresolved, can propagate erroneous assumptions upon which life decisions are then improperly based. In actuality, Truth is never contradictory or confusing, but straightforward and complete, supporting itself, as well as all of existence. The more familiar one becomes with the unchanging Word of God, the more that quandaries about both God and life are cleared up, providing greater understanding.

The questions that are raised, though, are themselves important to resolving confusion. Provoking thought, they can initiate research, considerations and conversations that lead to greater comprehension. Even though in this life no man except Jesus (see John 16:30) will ever know all, an investigative study of the Bible's verses provides knowledge that can translate via God-given insight into life altering enlightenment. Benefits can be not only long lasting, but everlasting, with positive effects rippling through future generations.

*The Life of the Cross*, the first book of *The Cross* series of books, opened with a question that had issued forth from the heart of my friend as we stood atop a mountain, gazing down upon the world below us. She had asked the question that dwells in and among us all: *How can God allow so much pain and suffering to exist in a world that is so beautiful?*

Her question embodies all of the other questions presented above and more. We all want to know that if God exists, then what kind of God is He to both create indescribable magnificence and tolerate indescribable destruction. We want answers to the questions that will explain the mysteries of life's meaning, giving peace of mind by making sense of both good times and bad. We want to know life's purpose, for without purpose, we simply exist for a short period of time, and then we are gone.

Recently, I received an answer from God to a personal question about which I had pondered along this line since the completion of my first book. The question was with regard to the purpose of the writing of my books, for I am aware that their purpose and mine are inseparable. Not until I was nearing the conclusion of the sixth book, however, did an answer come. Descriptive in nature, it arrived, delivering understanding in the same manner by which God has at other times also revealed information to me. This time He succinctly said, *"A trail of crumbs from the Bread of Life that has been fed to you."*

*The Cross* series of books, of which this book is a part, is the record of my God-led journey into the Truth of God's Word that is delivering personal peace in restoration through knowledge of God. The words within the books reveal the progression of growing relationship with God and the greater understanding that personal revelation through knowledge develops. Laden with ongoing transformation, the books reveal the power of God actively working in and through one life by both word and deed. In testifying to experience, the books are spoken one word at a time relative to an unending progression of events, for fellowship with God, once initiated, is everlasting.

This book then, the seventh in the series, is the arrival point to which the others have been leading. My awareness at this moment, despite not yet knowing what is to be written, is that an answer to the initial question is forthcoming. The rationale that is to be presented will be one of present and growing insight that compiles previous enlightenment into a more cohesive, but still incomplete, whole. The work, begun and sustained by God, is without end, for each shared thought is like that of but a single frame of a movie that is still being shot and edited. More is yet to be developed.

The number seven, associated biblically with fullness and completion, appears more than five hundred times in the Bible. It first appears in conjunction with the completion of God's creation of the physical universe in Genesis 2 and then bows out with thirty-six final appearances in Revelation, the Bible's end.[1]

The number rocks of God being "the Alpha and the Omega, the Beginning and the End" (Revelation 21:6; see also Revelation 1:8, 22:13). In our eternal God, time does not exist, for God is God forever, beyond all time. In Him, beginnings and endings are one

---

[1] [1] Zondervan. "Keyword Search / Search Results for 'seven.'" BibleGateway. www.biblegateway.com (accessed June 16, 2016).

and the same, for all life cycles to completeness through God. Summed up, God is All.

In writing this book, I am to be led further down the trail that God has blazed for me to follow to completion. This book and the others in the series are recording mechanisms, designed to hold the specific glimpses of God that He hands to me to share with others. The glimpses help all who will choose to consider their content to better distinguish between the everlasting and the fleeting, empowering lives with greater Truth that more fully reflects God's glory.

With beginnings and endings intertwining, there is no telling, except by God, of what is yet to come. Willingness to follow God's lead is imperative to receiving life's blessings that God has planned to give through His perfecting of our knowledge of the Truth. Of this, I am certain: *faith increases in the unfolding of the Truth of God, creating peace.*

Even when our faith walk with God begins at some skeptical distance from Him, the Word of God draws us closer to God's side at a pace conducive to our individual comfort levels and positioning within His Word. Every exposure to God's Word delivers progression in our relationships with God, continually moving us closer to Him. Over time, a metaphorical hand-holding trust of God develops that enables us to walk through life in more uniform step with Him.

A mature faith, though, is acquired only when the Truth of God becomes so engrained in us that we release our hand-hold of

God to be lifted upon His shoulders. In that position alone, carried along fully by God, is our walk of faith effortless in terms of propulsion and right on track. From that height, we can more clearly see the route that lies ahead, giving us a better view of our final destination. This is the position of faith to which God desires us all to be delivered.

God has issued a standing invitation to every individual, asking all to choose to join in the fellowship of the Body of Christ, unifying our journeys through this life into the next by adherence to the Word of God. All who respond experience a road trip like no other; for along the way, we are immersed in a camaraderie that defies worldly explanation, as we are made more fully aware of just how much our good God loves us all.

So, how good is God's goodness, and how great is His love? The questions are universal, but answers vary, though they shouldn't, dividing denominations and even families in strife that all can agree is neither good nor loving.

How are we to know the Truth, then, if personal experiences and opinions vary? The only way is to personally follow the trail of evidence that God has supplied, opening our minds and hearts to *receive* more of the Truth that God reveals.

Far more than truthful, *God is Truth...* beginning to end, period.

# *The Strategizing* (God Almighty)

Sometimes the beginning of something is better understood from the vantage point of its ending. Considering that, let us begin by looking at the bottom-line: the Bible's end.

But first, two assumptions previously affirmed in other books of *The Cross* series must be acknowledged. One, God exists; two, He actively participates in men's lives. With that said, the questions revolving around God's love and goodness remain. What does *agape* (the New Testament Greek word for God's perfect love) look like in terms of goodness? How does it play out in men's lives? Can man truly depend upon God to always act in his best interest? If so, what does *best interest* even mean? How do men's existences and deaths tie in to God's supposed goodness and love? Why does God appear to be so different in the Old Testament than in the New Testament, and what is God like today?

The questions are not merely academic. Their perceived answers, correct or not, are crucial, for they fashion men's relationships with God by determining how willing men are to interact with Him. Alluding to this fact, a man has been quoted as having once said how glad he is that he learned of God's goodness before he learned of God's greatness.

To be aware of God's great power, but not His goodness, can create an inappropriate anxiety-producing fear of God, instead of reverential fear that rightly honors Him. Such fear can cause men to draw back from God, keeping a self-estimated "safe" distance away in uncertainty of God's true character and nature, as well as in not knowing what God might yet do.

Men's varying interpretations of the Bible's declarations that "No one is good--except God alone" (Mark 10:18; Luke 18:19) and that "God is love" (1 John 4:8, 16) can affect every aspect of life. Expectation that God will yet do good or not in any present or future situation is based to a large degree on personal knowledge of God and the way in which we interpret past experience (or lack of) with Him. Right knowledge can lead to proclaiming, "Those who know your name will trust in you, for you, LORD, have never forsaken those who seek you" (Psalm 9:10).

The Book of Revelation, in disclosing the final results of God's plan in this world, removes anxiety that uncertainty produces. Boiled down, the book reveals that evil is expunged, never to rise again, and that God's Family moves in to live with Him permanently, never to leave Home again. The loss and gain equate to one vast gain, for the end of all evil includes a purpose of fully protecting all God's Kingdom from ever suffering again. The welfare of God's Family is God's great concern forever. His goodness is eternal, prevailing over all, apart from both time and mankind's lack of knowledge of the Truth (see Revelation 19-22).

Even though a good degree of relief is offered by the knowledge that the end of Revelation reveals, questions about God's goodness in this world can still be perplexing. If God is so concerned about protecting mankind from all evil, then why hasn't He simply wiped evil out, alleviating pain and grief long before now? He certainly has the power (ability) to do so, doesn't He? Why did He even permit evil to exist in the first place? How could evil's presence in the world be good in any way, shape or form?

Throughout the Bible, both God's desire and His ability to deal with evil are plainly visible. But nowhere are they more affirmed than in John's vision in Revelation, when John was shown that "death and Hades were thrown into the lake of fire" (Revelation 20:14). But some two thousand years after the vision was *given* to John, the promised event has not yet materialized. With the passing of each additional moment, confusion among men increases as to why God is delaying so long in fulfilling that which is so good. Many can't help but believe that, *given* God's power to act accordingly, they would end all evil right here and now without hesitation. So if God is indeed the one true standard against which all goodness and love are measured, then why hasn't He done so?

Though the world is still waiting for the Bible's ending to occur, a finish line is in sight. The Bible, though appearing at first glance to be a collection of disjointed stories, is one continuous historical event. All of the accounts between the opening and closing pages unite to present a big picture view of the ongoing, developing relationship between God and man.

But those same pages also shed light on how the individual detailed pieces of the puzzle concerning life and death fit together in unity with the whole. Through Holy Spirit guidance within God's Word, understanding comes as connections are made between specific details, generating insight. But, additionally, God also provides insight at times by drawing parallels between the Bible's Truth and everyday occurrences with which men are more familiar, such as Jesus often did in telling parables.

With that end purpose in mind, consider the scenario that opens Paramount Pictures' 1982 fictional movie *Star Trek II: The Wrath of Khan*. In the movie, the character of Admiral James T. Kirk is aboard the *USS Enterprise*, a Federation starship charged with both exploration of the universe and the protection of all life within the universe. Having at one time captained the *Enterprise*, Kirk is onboard to oversee the *Kobayashi Maru* test that is being given to officer trainees.

In the test, a civilian ship is hypothetically marooned in a treaty-designated neutral zone that exists between the Federation (the movie's good guys) and their arch enemy, the Klingons. Each trainee, captaining the *Enterprise* in simulation only during the test, must choose either to disregard the treaty, illegally entering the neutral zone to rescue the civilians, or to follow protocol by remaining outside of the neutral zone, thereby abandoning the powerless civilian ship to hopelessness.

The trainee is well aware that breaking the treaty will initiate war with the waiting Klingons, who will have a legal right to fire upon the *Enterprise*, blowing the ship to smithereens. But if the trainee chooses not to attempt to save the civilian ship, the ship's passengers will definitively die. The test is considered to be a no-win proposition that is meant to prepare trainees for just such future moral choices that they will encounter in real life situations.

The storyline goes that, in every prior administration of the test but one, the outcome of the simulation was always as expected: at least one of the two ships was destroyed. But once, and only once, the situation that was thought to be impossible to win was overcome to bring about the safe deliverance of both ships. That single success was accomplished by a young James T. Kirk, who never believed in no-win scenarios.

After having failed the test twice, Kirk had then secretly inserted a subroutine into the test's computer program the night before he was to take the test again. Then the next day, during the test, when the time was right, he was able to employ the routine that only he knew existed. Thereby he achieved the desired result: victory over death.

While some people called his actions dishonest, James T. Kirk was commended by others for his bold ingenuity and his refusal to give up. When he was given no way to achieve success, *he made a way by planning ahead for the situation that he knew was coming.*

Refusing to walk into the trap that the test laid out, Kirk implanted an escape route that he kept secret until the time came to employ its benefit. Imagine the shocked look that would have appeared on the faces of all who would have been present during Kirk's test, as they witnessed the unexpected conclusion!

Now, returning to reality, imagine the similar though far greater stunned looks that must have occurred on the faces of those who personally witnessed the resurrected Jesus! His defeat of a real-life scenario that appeared to be a no-win situation amazed not only those who were present and saw the resurrected Jesus for themselves, but also a world full of people, who would eventually hear and believe the Truth through the testimonies that would be shared by them and others (see John 20:29).

Jesus' life-giving resurrection followed a dilemma that was similar in nature to the *Kobayashi Maru* test. (The word *dilemma*, though an oxymoron relative to God's all-knowing wisdom, is being used here for discussion purposes.)

The dilemma began in the Garden of Eden, where God had first visibly revealed His goodness and love in the beauty of a world that He personally proclaimed six times to be "good" (Genesis 1:4, 9, 12, 18, 21, 25) and another time even "very good" (Genesis 1:31). Following Creation's completion, God then presented the good world that He had made to Adam---mankind (man), as a gift. Having created man in His own image for fellowship with him, God entrusted man with dominion over the Earth that was God's to freely give (see Genesis 1:26-30).

Along with the authority that accompanied dominion, though, came responsibility. Man's successful leadership (management) of his domain depended upon two factors: always acting in the best interest of the world that was in his care and always properly deferring to the higher authority of God, who always knows best.

But sometime after man *received* his domain, he mismanaged on both counts. He chose to act in a way that he thought was in his own best interest, rather than that of the world, and he also chose to ignore God's warning not to do so. With little, if any, forethought as to what he was relinquishing, man simply handed dominion of the Earth over to Satan. He neglected his responsibility to care for the world that had been entrusted to him. Instead of being grateful for what he did have, he obsessed about getting the one thing that he did not have:  knowledge of good and evil. So he went after it, hoping to achieve godly status. By acting self-centeredly, man failed the world that was in his care. He failed to rightly value the privilege of caring for the world that God so loved.

The world's change in regimes resulted when Satan, using words of ammunition that intentionally questioned the words of God, fired a shot of temptation at Eve, Adam's helpmate, who was part of the world that was in man's care (see Genesis 1:26, 2:19-25). Together, the two (mankind) deliberated little in deciding individually to each surrender their lives to Satan (see Genesis 3:1-7).

When Satan asked the ever tempting question, "Did God really say ... ?" (Genesis 3:1b), mankind *took* the bait hook, line and sinker to be firmly caught in temptation's trap. By aligning with Satan to doubt God, man separated himself from God. He broke the fellowship of trust with God that God had established with him.

Man exchanged loyalty to God for self-promotion. He committed the same sin of pride as had Satan (see Genesis 3; Isaiah 14:12-15; Ezekiel 28:12-19).

Once man had broken his relationship with God, he was powerless to repair it. Stranded by his own deliberate poor choice, he had become part of an ongoing battle in which evil continued *taking* one pot shot after another at men who were not good at ducking (see Ephesians 6:12). No longer did all appear in God's good Creation to be as good as it once had been.

Evil---opposition to the Truth of God, once unleashed in man, multiplied freely, enveloping the world. Satan himself, however, remained limited. Not a god, he is neither all-knowing nor all-powerful and can only be in one place at a time. Simply stated, Satan, like man, is a created being who chose to attempt to magnify himself instead of God. Having stood face-to-face with God, as well as having been *given* sufficient intelligence and information to have chosen wisely, Satan (again like man) had ample knowledge and opportunity to rightly humble himself before God, his Creator. But he didn't. Disrupting life's natural order, he tried to live an imagined equality to God that backfired on him, as man's similar attempt to do so also backfired on man.

But despite his limitations, Satan appeared to have God over a barrel, so to speak. Though God had the power to take back the Earth from Satan forcefully, He had no legal right by His own righteousness to do so (see Jeremiah 23:6). He had deeded the Earth to man, who had deeded it to Satan. Reclaiming the Earth as His own would have to be done justly, for it is impossible for God to be unrighteous. God cannot sin.

God's dilemma was this: Not only did evil rule the world, but man was corrupted by the sin that had taken root *in* him. If God wiped evil from the face of the Earth, then man, who could not separate himself from his sin, would be destroyed along with it.

Facing the original and granddaddy of all *Kobayashi Maru*-type tests, what could God, wanting only good for all people do (see Jeremiah 29:11)? If God did nothing, man was doomed to die by the sin that infected him, for "the wages of sin is death" (Romans 6:23a). On the other hand, if God wiped all sinfulness from the Earth, man would be destroyed in the process. From Satan's point of view, God appeared to be caught in a no-win scenario. Evil appeared to have the upper hand.

Had God been anyone other than God, that most probably would have been the case. But being God, God knew not only the end from the beginning, but also every point in between. God has never been surprised by any development (see Isaiah 46:8-10).

What if, unbeknownst to Creation, God's divine wisdom had prepared ahead of time for the very dilemma that had developed? That would change the entire scenario, wouldn't it? Well, that is exactly what did happen. In a move similar to Kirk adding an escape plan to the *Kobayashi Maru* simulation program, God inserted an escape route of His making into His Creation plan, *an escape route that would specifically save mankind and the world from the sin that God knew was coming.*

Before time began, God planned ahead (see John 1:1-4), rightly choosing to build Creation on the foundation of Jesus Christ (see 1 Corinthians 3:11). Jesus would be the One and Only Way out of death and into the life with God that God had planned for man (see John 14:6). As a result of Jesus' boldness and perseverance in suffering the penalty of sin for man, no sin-burdened person would ever need to perish (See Romans 10:13).

Jesus has always been man's eternal light of hope (see John 1:4-5, 8:12). Because of God's loving-goodness, man has never been hopeless, but simply ignorant---*unknowing of the full measure of God's love and goodness.* Had God ever been less than unchangeable perfection (see Psalm 18:30; James 1:17), not having perfectly provided for every need, as He has indeed done for beyond all time (see Genesis 22:14; Philippians 4:19), this discourse would not exist. But because of God's constancy (see Hebrews 13:8), man has a Savior, who is delivering men forever into greater knowledge of the Truth (see Colossians 1:9-14).

Jesus Christ---"Christ in you" (Colossians 1:27)---was to be God's mystery kept hidden until the proper time when Jesus' righteousness would be employed to redeem (purchase back) the world from Satan (Ephesians 3:2-12). Then men would see that "God so loved the world that he gave his one and only son" (John 3:16a). The transaction would be one of a kind, using the blood of Jesus as God's due payment for sin (see Revelation 5:9).

Leaving nothing to chance, only choice, God created potential in the Garden of Eden for a winning scenario no matter which tree's fruit mankind would choose to eat (see Genesis 2:8-17). Either way, by eating the fruit of the Tree of Life (the immediate route to the ongoing life that is in Jesus) or by eating the fruit of the Tree of the Knowledge of Good and Evil (the longer route), God's loving-goodness would do no less than freely grant man the opportunity to enjoy everlasting life with God. God would *give* His best to all men, always acting in their best interest right from the beginning.

If mankind declined God's first offer of life via the Tree of Life, the alternate route would still fulfill God's good and perfect will for man. Man could still live with God, if he would *accept* the help of his God, who was at hand, providing for all of mankind's needs. If man overlooked or bypassed the Tree of Life in the Garden of Eden for any reason, neither comprehending its good provision nor being satisfied with its availability, then the Cross (the other Tree of Life), would be waiting via the Tree of the Knowledge of Good and Evil to *give* men the understanding that would *give* them life everlasting by God's salvation plan.

Either way, only one way existed for man to *receive* life, and that way was by the uncompromising grace of God that would refuse not to provide in accordance with God's righteousness and man's needs. As time would affirm, the life offered to man as a gift from God could be neither earned nor achieved by man's efforts, but only *received* by grace through faith in God (see Romans 5:2; Ephesians 2:8).

God alone is capable of supplying mankind with the provision that is needed to convince men of the Truth that *gives* life. Everything---*everything*---in life depends upon the loving-goodness of God's righteous provision that is *given* by grace. God holds back no good thing in doing eternal good to meet all need. Above all and for all, He has even *given* His beloved Son.

Far more than providing, *God is Provision...* beginning to end, period.

# *The Choosing* (Adam/Man)

God is eternal life (see 1 John 5:20). He Self-exists as Father, Son and Holy Spirit. He is One God (see Mark 12:29), without external limitation. Yet within God's eternity, God has placed time, marking the development of Creation. Born from God's Eternal Word, Creation came forth from God as multi-faceted light (see Genesis 1:1-3; John 1:1-5), for "God is light" (1 John 1:5b). The light that God sent shed God's enlightenment over all.

Enlightenment---*knowledge of the Truth of God*---is embedded in all physical and spiritual existence. Merely by being, God's Creation glorifies God, *giving* no man excuse for not worshipping God (see Romans 1:20). But to the never ending increasing glory of God, men have been *given* the ability to absorb more fully the realization of the glory due God in limitless and timeless glorification of Him. But connected to that ability is the gift of free will, freeing men to worship God or not.

Free will is a gift of extreme freedom emanating from the extreme love and grace of God. Complete unto Himself, God is sovereign. But within His sovereignty, He has freely chosen to freely share Himself with Creation, *giving* Himself fully to all.

Measured against God, man's imperfection stands out as need (lack). Designed by God to be in need of Him, men are not gods in and of themselves. But rather, in being made in God's image (see Genesis 1:26-27), men are the further complementation of God's perfection. As such, men have the God-*given* ability to *receive* from God. Being eternal Source, God is forever pouring out, and He has made men to be everlasting recipients of His generosity. The gift of need leads to men *receiving* the Gift of God.

But a gift is only a gift if it is both freely *given* and freely *received*. In choosing to *give* enlightenment, God honors men with opportunity to grow to be more like Him. In turn, the act of *receiving* from God rightly acknowledges men's continual need of God, who always has more to *give*. Thereby, *acceptance* of godly enlightenment worships God. On the other hand, men's refusal to *receive* enlightenment from God is a metaphorical slap in the face that dishonors God by wrongly denying need of Him.

The concept and implementation of worship through enlightened choice are phenomenal. Beyond awesome, they are producing in totality a Creation that is in continual upward-spiraling transformation, forever expanding the magnification of God's great glory.

In the Garden of Eden, where God walked freely with man, revealing Himself to man, God *gave* man full access to the enlightenment for which man was made. There God placed the Tree of Life, brimming with the Truth of God. As long as man obeyed God, he had full access to the Truth, because he had full access to

God. He was with God in the Garden, and he could remain there, fully enjoying life by choosing to continue curbing his appetite with the fruit of any tree except the off limit one.

As long as man rightly did so, he honored God and order remained intact, strengthening man's right relationship with God. The Truth of God that would one day be revealed to mankind through Jesus was made available to man right from the beginning in multiplicity. No good thing was withheld from him, including the opportunity to live with God in the Garden forever. The availability of God's abundant grace was prolific.

In that perfect Garden setting, man stood out as being different from the remainder of the Creation that surrounded him, for he was able to grow in a way that nothing else could. His ability to acquire knowledge of both God and himself made his dependence upon God more intimate than that of the rest of Creation. The ability was *given* to him as means of filling the need for God that God had placed within him. In both drawing man to Himself and enabling man to continue growing closer to Him, God made provision for a win-win scenario.

But to grow in intimacy with God, man must both acknowledge his need for God and allow God to fulfill that need by *receiving* Truth from Him. *Receiving* fulfills need, affirming proper relationship. It also further develops man's trust of God. Greater trust results in yet increased *receiving* and closeness, further deepening the relationship. God's desire to share more of Himself in ongoing fellowship with man and man's need for God are designed to be mutually fulfilling, *giving* only pleasure.

The faith in God that man needs to continue in the cycle of fellowship was never designed to be blind faith, but rather faith that is based on personal knowledge of God. Trust in God comes from man's understanding of who God is, of knowing God's character and nature. Accurate personal knowledge of God leads to man's greater understanding of God that then fuels greater trust, maintaining right order in right relationship.

Faith to trust God, though, is necessary only for those things that are needed, but are not yet seen, are not yet in hand (see Romans 8:24). So in order to develop man's faith in God, God *gave* man what was needed most: God *gave* His Word.

Right from the beginning of God's relationship with man, God warned that a lack of faith in His words would lead to certain death. God specifically told Adam in the Garden of Eden that if Adam disregarded God's warning and ate from the Tree of the Knowledge of Good and Evil, then Adam would surely die (see Genesis 2:17). God's words, of course, proved true. Man's disregard of God's good instruction dishonored God, breaking the relationship of trust between the two. Disconnecting from God, man relinquished life support. Unable to live, he was sure to die.

When man ate the forbidden fruit of disobedience, he digested self-awareness, making it the center point of his thinking from then on. As a result, his focus shifted from God to himself. At that moment, man fell from grace and into death, for he could not create the life that he needed. What he created instead was chaos in God's divine order of Creation.

Right in the middle of freely *receiving* the abundance of God's good Garden provision, man pushed aside whatever appreciation he had for his many blessings in order to zero in on the one thing that he did not have. As soon as he realized that he was without a particular something, he *took* offense that he did not have everything. Idiomatically speaking, man selfishly wanted the greener pasture that he thought was being withheld from him, and he was even willing to gamble away life to get it. Blinded by desire, he could only envision that there was more to life than that which he had been *given*, and he wanted "it," whatever "it" was. He wanted "it all," including the self-gratification of his self-sufficiency in attaining "it."

The temptation that led man to his downfall was one of self-promotion that came not from Satan, but from within him. While it promised him a lie, it led him to Truth, for the potential gain that he envisioned never panned out as he imagined. The knowledge that the forbidden fruit allotted man was indeed an eye-opener, but in a way that he had not anticipated. Instead of making him like God, as he was so led to believe that it would do (see Genesis 3:5), his sin only proved that he was not much like God at all. In actuality, his decision distanced him from God, to whom he should have been drawing closer, *not because God moved away from him, but because he moved away from God.* God remained ever-present and ever-providing. God was good, and man was not. The self-realization wasn't pretty.

In failing to comprehend the implications of his sin beforehand, man wrote himself into a no-win *Kobayashi Maru*-type dilemma. Worse, in his helpless state, he had no way of changing the script. Once he had distanced himself from God's righteousness by sinning, he had no way of returning---*reconciling*---himself to his former position with God, for he could not erase the sin that made him unrighteous (see Psalm 51:1-5; Romans 8:7-8).

The sudden realization of his sin caused man to be ashamed (see Genesis 3:7-13). Caught off-guard by the awareness, he vainly attempted to hide from all-knowing God. Then, when confronted by the One against whom he had indeed sinned, he fed his shame all the more by futilely trying to blame his sin on another. Fact was, he couldn't bear to face himself, for he had thought himself better than that which sin had revealed him to be.

God, though, in knowing man fully, was not surprised in the least by him. So a good God stood by, ready to rightly help sinful man, despite having suffered man's betrayal. Incapable of failure, God would prove His way right, for He is never wrong. Life would be restored the right way, the only way, by God's loving-goodness that would remain firm, even amidst wrongful death (see Isaiah 53).

Far more than righteous, *God is Righteousness*... beginning to end, period.

# The Remaining (Cain)

Following man's fall from grace, a righteous God had to necessarily usher unrighteous mankind out of the Garden of Eden and into the difficult life that man had unwittingly chosen for himself. But before man departed from the Garden, God first enlightened him to the nature of his new life, *giving* him an overview of the life that lay ahead (see Genesis 3:14-19).

The curse that came upon both man and the ground as a result of man's sin was not punishment, but consequence that would instruct. It was an integral component of the route to returning mankind to everlasting life with God. The fruitless sweat and pain that would be experienced apart from God would be the driving force used to turn man's prideful thinking right.

But the process would require time. As pride had tripped man up within the Garden of Eden, pride would continue to be man's downfall outside, as well. As long as man would keep trying to prove his capabilities sufficient for his need, his pride would stand in the way of him *receiving* the full blessings of life that God had waiting for him. As an obstacle standing between God and man, pride was going to have to *take* a fall of its own.

When God had first placed man in the Garden of Eden, He had *given* man responsibility for the Garden's care (see Genesis 2:15). In being so honored by God, man had reaped the Garden's harvest of benefits for some time before *giving* it all away. The Garden ground that had been his domain had been blessed with life's fullness by God's very Presence.

But the ground that man came to work outside of the Garden was different ground. Cursed by sin, it was Satan's territory (see Genesis 3:17). No matter how much man toiled or strove, trying to prove self-sufficiency, his results were far from perfect. Even his best efforts, limited by God's perfect design of him, had to fall short of God's perfection. Man couldn't replicate the Garden life with God that God had freely provided. Life in a world that was Satan's domain would be hard.

But as disheveled as the world would yet become by evil's rule, God would remain righteously loyal to all Creation, loving it continuously (see John 3:16). God would not permit evil to have its way on the Earth forever. When God escorted man from the Garden of Eden and then blocked the Garden's entrance with "cherubim and a flaming sword flashing back and forth ..." (Genesis 3:24a), He did so for the good of the entire world. More specifically, He did so "... to guard the way to the tree of life" (Genesis 3:24b).

The same God, who had previously *given* man free access to the Tree of Life, chose to bar man from even approaching it. Why? Was an angry God punishing man for sin? Was a holy God being vengeful? Did a good God no longer love no-good man?

Time would reveal that God was angry, but not as man tends to reason. God was angry for man's sake, not in opposition to him. God's action was indeed just, for it opposed the demise of His good Creation. It set a limit to sin's existence, not to the existence of the men infected by sin. More than any loving earthly parents could ever care for their children, God cared for His. He did so, knowing that their pain and suffering had been completely avoidable, had they only respected Him by obeying His words.

Though a more comprehensive answer to the question regarding God's action of barring man from the Garden commands consideration of individual aspects of the totality of God's character (love, righteousness, justice, mercy, faithfulness, etc.), contemplate the following. What would the world look like today, let alone an eon from now, had sinful man eaten from the Tree of Life and never died, but had continued propagating more sinful people forever?

Setting aside practical concerns, such as overpopulation, think of the effects of evil's multiplication. How much evil could the world contain before becoming a living hell, a nightmare from which man could never awaken? That kind of suffering would be needless... without divine purpose... anything but good.

By denying sinful man access to the Tree of Life, God continued to both fully love man and fully sustain His own righteousness. With one rightful denial, God did good, helping all men. He prevented evil from having an unending rule on the Earth that would have maximized man's suffering and minimized the good that man would ever be able to know.

Good and evil are mutually exclusive. They are the antithesis of one another. Evil is not of God, but only exists apart from Him. Righteousness and unrighteousness, being polar opposites, do not cohabitate. Every being is either righteous (good) or unrighteous (evil).

In Garden of Eden days, man had been deemed good by God. Yet man had no rules to live by, save the one regarding the Tree of the Knowledge of Good and Evil. Whatever man did or did not do in his day-to-day living, he was completely *accepted* by God, just as he was. Man was good simply by his connection to God, who is the definition of goodness.

Simply stated, God is good, and Satan is evil. What God *gives*, Satan *takes*, and that includes life. What God builds, Satan destroys, and that includes relationships. What God loves, Satan hates, and that includes mankind.

Though evil presents an appearance of strength, it has a weak spot that makes it easy to target effectively. Man's error in missing the target is that he attempts to oppose evil with more evil, which only strengthens evil by adding to it. Evil's only hope of survival is in deceiving men into *accepting* its ways over those of God. God alone, always righteously good, knows the weakness that destroys evil: *in doing good, evil is undone.*

Overcoming evil really is as simple as doing good. When men side with God, emulating His goodness, evil backs down (see 1 Peter 5:8-9). It must, for without reinforcement, it is doomed to fade. By *taking* a stand on God's Word in support of Truth, men are upheld by God's strength to put evil down. But without God's Word, men are easy prey for lies and deception that do evil (see 2 Timothy 3:13), even when they masquerade as good (see 2 Corinthians 11:14).

Regardless of appearances, which men often misinterpret, God has been combatting and defeating evil with the goodness of His every word and deed since before He even spoke Creation into being. God's banishment of man from the Garden was not punishment, per se, but a necessary consequence of sin entering man. As the world's first recorded example of moral tough love, the banishment was done in man's best interest.

The evidence indicating that God was still for man and not against him following man's fall is this: though man had to leave the Garden, God didn't leave man. God continued conversing with man, *giving* him needed guidance and direction, loving him in the precise way that he best needed to be loved.

Cain, the firstborn son of Adam and Eve, is a specific case in point (see Genesis 4:1-16). When Cain wrongfully grew jealous of his brother, Abel, God told Cain that, unless Cain mastered the sin within him, sin would master him. God wanted Cain to know that his sinful nature, inherited through his father's seed (see Romans 5:12), was what Cain needed to be fighting, not his brother. God knew what Cain was about to learn: sin is a formidable opponent that, when given license, stops at nothing to *take* all that it wants.

Despite being forewarned by God, Cain fell prey to sin's power of persuasion. Enmeshed in wrong desires, Cain became a victim of evil by agreeing to be its perpetrator. Driven by wrong thinking and corresponding emotions, Cain *took* matters regarding his brother into his own hands, tearing apart the family that God had formed. In surrendering to sin, Cain made his life an instrument of death. He *took* his brother's life, making Abel pay for what Cain wanted: revenge. But the cost of sin proved to be far more than either of them could afford.

Whatever satisfaction Cain *took* in his brother's death proved to be short-lived. Cain's real problem had never been with his brother, but was in him. When the deadly deed of sin was over and done, sinfulness still remained. The act of sinning did not quench the sinfulness in Cain, but only reinforced it, adding to his guilt.

Burdened by the knowledge that he had sinned against both God and man, Cain feared a vengeance that could *take* his life in retribution for the one that he had *taken*. Cain had spilled his brother's blood upon the Earth, and the blood that had *given* life to his brother was crying out to God for justice (see Genesis 4:10), for "the life of every creature is its blood" (Leviticus 17:14).

In years to come, much blood would be spilled by man's many acts of anger and revenge, draining the world of God-*given* life. But the day would come when Jesus would promise that all spilled blood would be rightly avenged (see Matthew 23:35). Sacrificially, Jesus would pour out His own blood, transfusing His life into a dying world. He would be God's justice---a justice that would include compassionate mercy that is necessary for life's sustainment (see Zechariah 7:9). Whereas Cain had tried to gain self-satisfaction by *taking* life from another, Jesus would have satisfaction in *giving* His life to all others.

During the years, though, before Jesus would deliver God's good and loving mercy to a hurting world, God would continue *giving* His mercy to men in a myriad of other ways. Cain *received* it in a mark that God placed upon his forehead, protecting him from a revengeful death. In *giving* Cain the specific undeserved gift that he needed, God kept him from *receiving* the death that he feared that he deserved by men's accounting. God was good and loving to Cain, not because Cain measured up in any way (he didn't and couldn't), but because God always meets His own standard of perfection.

Loving Cain perfectly, God freely *gave* Cain exactly what Cain needed, for God so loved the murdering Cain equally as much as He so loved the murdered Abel and every other man who would ever come to be (see John 3:16). Cain had failed to understand that fact when he and Abel had presented their offerings to God, for while Abel's had been found to be rightly offered from the heart, Cain's had been found to be lacking. While Cain had kept the best of his bounty for himself, Abel had *given* the best of his flock to God. Cain's mediocre offering was not in itself Cain's problem, but, rather, was indicative of a problem in his heart.

God knew where Cain's selfish withholding would lead, and He didn't want Cain to go that route. He didn't want Cain to experience the pain and suffering that selfishness creates. But free to choose, Cain went there anyway, and still God faithfully *gave* Cain exactly what he needed in order for Cain to continue living. When God mercifully touched Cain, He proved that His care for Cain extended beyond sin's reach.

While mankind vacillates between choosing to do good and evil, God does not, for He cannot. God is the same yesterday, today and forever (see Hebrews 13:8). God can be only faithfully consistent in the application of His good and loving righteousness, for God is God forever, loving perfectly without exception. Every word and deed of God proves Him faithful, even to the extent that He freely enters into covenant with men who are not.

Far more than faithful, *God is Faithfulness*... beginning to end, period.

# *The Preparing* (God the Father)

Time would substantiate God's faithfulness. It would also allow for the gradual conversion of men's thinking from that of unyielding pride to that of humble submission to God. Opinionated on every subject, men would be slow to learn that trying to prove that they are right is of no everlasting value, but that allowing God to make them right is. Mere babes in their knowledge of God, men would have a lot of maturing to do, and God---perfect Father---would be the One to raise them up right.

The Family that God had first brought to life in the Garden of Eden had left Home on a sour note. In essence, they had *given* up their Garden inheritance to go to work for themselves. Their imaginations, fueled by temptation's words, had run wild, and they had decided to go along for the ride to see just how far they could get on their own. When their dreams fell flat, they were left stranded. Not only did they need a lift Home, they didn't even know which way to go to get there.

Men only have two choices regarding where they can spend eternity: with God in His Home or with Satan in his hell. Hell is a location designated by God as an everlasting holding tank for all evil---everything separated from God. It is where Satan and other demons will permanently dwell amid their own torment (see Matthew 25:41; Revelation 20:10). God's desire is that no man would ever know hell's torture, but would avoid hell at all cost, even the cost to God of His Son. God implores all men to choose life, not death, for it is men's choice to make (see Deuteronomy 30:19). God "wants all men to be saved and to come to a knowledge of the truth" (1 Timothy 2:4).

When sin entered man in the Garden of Eden, life on the Earth began deteriorating. Disorder affected every aspect of this fallen world, including everything from man's genetic makeup to the Earth's plate tectonics. Nothing was spared. Spiritual battles (see Daniel 10:12-14) overflowed into the lives of men (see Ephesians 6:10-18), luring men into battling one another.

Men, who should have been fighting in alliance with God, weren't. Their ineptness at even recognizing evil, let alone overcoming it, kept them down and out by all counts but that of God. God knew the final score that would be tallied at just the right time in the enacting of His escape plan: Jesus---the One whom He had waiting to not only fight for man, but also as a man.

But in the world's downward spiraling condition, the future appeared bleak. The more that men tried to achieve worldly gain, the more spiritual ground they seemed willing to *give* up to get it.

However, "with God all things are possible" (Matthew 19:26; Mark 10:27; Luke 18:27). In God's perfect timing, God the Father would reveal Jesus to be "the way and the truth and the life" (John 14:6a). Jesus would be men's way Home to God. Jesus, though, would always *give* credit where due, saying, "... it is the Father, living in me, who is doing his work" (John 14:10b).

Not only would Jesus be God's only salvation plan for men, He would also be the best God could ever offer anyone. Once God the Father would reveal Himself to mankind in Jesus Christ, He would have nothing better to *give* to the world. Jesus---God's Son---is God's quintessential Gift, an all-or-nothing peace offering. Jesus is each man's opportunity to choose life or death---God or hell---for himself, no matter how far from Home he finds himself to be when he realizes that he is stranded.

Due to the gravity of the decision to be made by all men, God has allotted all of time to best preparing men to choose wisely. Systematically, God continually develops men's faith in Him, one step at a time (see Ephesians 2:8; 2 Thessalonians 1:3). Time is crucial in God's plan, and He has allotted "a time for everything, and a season for every activity under heaven" (Ecclesiastes 3:1). Each moment has been *given* designated purpose that fulfils specific need. Not a moment is wasted; not a one goes by without God using it for good. Even as Adam and Eve were being escorted out of the Garden of Eden, the clock was ticking up to salvation, according to God's perfect timing.

But until salvation would arrive, *giving* hope, man would consume time with increasing sinfulness. Sin consciousness, as well as actual sin, would become debilitating, isolating men mentally and emotionally, as well as spiritually, from God. So ashamed was man when he left the Garden of Eden that not again until the days of

Enosh (Adam's grandson through his son Seth), almost two and a half centuries later, did time and generations sufficiently distance man from past guilt to enable him to again begin calling on God (see Genesis 4:26b).

The lie that evil whispers to men's souls is that man is too sinful to be wanted by a holy God. The lie says that a man must first clean up his act and straighten himself out before he can seek God and ask God for help. The lie is designed to do what evil intends: to keep men helplessly separated from God. The lie fabricates a false god, one who expects men to match God's perfection. It depicts a god who is a harsh taskmaster and unforgiving by nature, one who is hard to please and considers men unworthy of His attention. It depicts a tyrannical and uncaring god who is out to get men who don't measure up.

Nothing could be further from the Truth of God. If men could be good enough to deserve God, they would be their own gods---complete unto themselves without any need for God. God delights in being God and in blessing men with His abundant goodness and love. Know this: "He who did not spare his own Son, but gave him up for us all---how will he not also, along with him, graciously give us all things?" (Romans 8:32).

A time would come in Jesus' ministry when He would tell a parable about a prodigal son (see Luke 15). When the son, who had previously *taken* his inheritance from his father and left home, finally returned home where he belonged, he arrived having come straight from a pigpen. There he had been sleeping and eating in addition to working, for he had foolishly squandered his inheritance on worthless thrills. Life on his own had not been what the son had expected. So when he arrived home, he was penniless, undoubtedly carrying an odor of dismal poverty that was anything but attractive.

Yet the father, ever watchful for his son's return, ran to meet his son when his son was still a long way off. Only grateful that his son was heading home, the father fully embraced his son, completely disregarding the son's uncleanness. The son was *received* back into the family that was forever his, and the father rejoiced unabashedly in his son's presence. The father delighted in having opportunity to lavish his love upon his son in ways that far exceeded his son's hope. By the son turning to his father for help, the son's need to *receive* from his father made provision for his father to *give*, while the father's desire to *give* to his son made provision for his son to *receive*. Family life, as designed by God, was restored in the *giving* that flowed from a father's love.

The story is about God's self-fulfilling family-style economy that is based on God's attributes as the perfect Father, attributes of love, forgiveness, grace, mercy, etc. As the father in the story is the son's only source of hope for survival, far more is God the Father mankind's only Source of hope (see Titus 3:7). In both cases, the father/Father provides abundant life, *giving* far more than necessity would dictate (see John 10:10). As the prodigal son most assuredly experienced after returning home to his father, mankind thrives in the Father's embrace, for there life is continually rekindled and kept ablaze by perpetual love.

Right from the beginning, God designed man for familial relationship, not isolation. Relationships are the only part of life in the physical world that men carry forward into the next. Having set the precedent for family life in the eternal, God replicates it in this world in man's best interest. He *gives* man a hungering for eternal Family. Eternal life provides eternal fellowship that meets every need. Isolation, on the other hand, creates suffering in eternal death that knows only ever-deepening deprivation apart from God.

Families, defined by God, are not merely a holdover from days gone by and, hence, no longer pertinent in today's society. They are God's vehicle for men *receiving* the full measure of His loving-goodness. Family life is foundational to eternal fellowship with God and one another in both this life and the next. Jesus is Creation's foundation (see John 1:3; 1 Corinthians 3:11) because He is the Father's Son upon whom the Family is built. As such, Jesus has a vested eternal interest---His life---in Family welfare. In *giving* His all, He never lets His Family down.

When the prodigal son declared independence from father and family to proudly strike out on his own, as mankind had similarly done with God, he cut himself off from his roots. Without roots, he lacked proper grounding, sustenance and support. One day, Jesus would explain the need for proper rooting another way.

> I am the vine. And you are the branches. If you remain in me and I in you, you will bear much fruit; apart from me, you can do nothing. (John 15:5)

Nothing... When cut off from Father and Family, man is malnourished. The worldly treats that he craves are, by nature, no more than the equivalent of junk food's empty calories. While their sweet taste may appeal to the senses, their bitter aftertaste makes them hard to swallow. In the end, smug self-gratification leads to self-loathing and contempt, leaving emptiness:  an unfulfilled void for God (see Ecclesiastes 3:11).

In the prodigal son's story, the father knew that his son, upon returning home, would need the proper nutrition that he had not been *receiving*. So while awaiting his son's return, the father had a calf fattened in advance of the celebration that he hoped would yet come. On a much grander scale, God also has similarly prepared a banquet in advance of His Family's homecoming celebration (see Revelation 19:9, 17; Luke 14:15-24).

But before beginning that banquet, God would use time to ready men to *accept* His invitation that He would extend to all men to join Jesus at the coming feast. Truth would be cultivated, weeding out doubt and fear that would otherwise keep men away, and tough love would be employed as necessary.

*Acceptance* would not come naturally to men. Rather, God would build *acceptance* in men, one step at a time.

- Before man could *accept* that salvation is by faith in Jesus, he would need to *accept* Jesus' resurrection to life eternal.

- Before that, man would need to *accept* that Jesus died and was buried.

- Before that, man would need to *accept* that the sin-free blood of Jesus paid the debt for sin that man owed God.

- Before that, man would need to *accept* Jesus' substitution for all men in suffering death on the Cross in their stead.

- Before that, man would need to *accept* that God would send a savior to redeem mankind.

- Before that, man would need to *accept* that redemption from sin comes through blood sacrifice.

- Before that, man would need to *accept* that life is contained in blood.

- Before that, man would need to *accept* that man's salvation could only come from God.

- Before that, man would need to *accept* that he cannot save himself from the death that sin delivers.

- Before that, man would need to *accept* that he is sinful from birth.

- Above all, man would need to *accept* that God is with and for him, not against him; that God is always good.

In God's salvation plan, the blood of the Son would *give* men access to a new inheritance, one of everlasting life through spiritual rebirth in Christ Jesus (see Romans 6:1-12). The rebirth would occur in confession of faith: a declaration of personal need for and *acceptance* of the salvation from sin and death that Jesus would provide (see Romans 10:9).

In *accepting* Jesus as Savior, men reborn into God's eternal Family would be *given* a new spirit and a new heart (see Ezekiel

36:26). Continually purified by Jesus' blood, the Family's bloodline could never again be tainted by sin. Each man's reconciliation to Father and Family would be permanent, dependent only upon the righteous position of Jesus: the firstborn Son of the Father (see Colossians 1:15).

Because God exists in eternity, apart from time, He is not restricted in any manner by time's confinements. Rather, He is omnipresent throughout time and location. When Jesus would pay for man's sin, God Omniscient would know every sin that man would ever incur against Him. Similar to paying the bill plus tip for a dinner before the meal is completely eaten, Jesus would overpay the full bill for all of mankind's sin throughout all time. God knew the debt's final tally that would be owed by all men before Adam and Eve ever came to first realize that they had sinned against God.

Likewise, though men's spiritual rebirths occur in specific moments, God has known each one since before time began (see Romans 8:28-30). God's Family, wanted by God, is well planned.

Rebirth is man's only means to becoming Family. Jesus would say that "no one can see the kingdom of God unless he is born again" (John 3:3b). In hearing that statement, Nicodemus, "a member of the Jewish ruling council" (John 3:1), who sought Truth in Jesus' day, would ask Jesus directly how such a feat could be accomplished. In responding, Jesus would expand upon the topic to say that "God did not send his Son into the world to condemn the world, but to save the world through him" (John 3:17).

The world was already condemned by sin. Cut off from God---life's Source, it needed to be reconnected and nourished well. It needed to *receive* "the Bread of Life" (John 6:35): Jesus Christ.

> I tell you the truth, unless you eat the flesh of the Son of Man and drink his blood, you have no life in you. Whoever eats my flesh and drinks my blood has eternal life, and I will raise him up at the last day. For my flesh is real food and my blood is real drink. Whoever eats my flesh and drinks my blood remains in me, and I in him. (John 6:53-56)

The communion table prepared by the Father would be where men, reborn by the Spirit, would partake freely of bread and wine (see Mark 14:22-25)---the Son's Body and Blood---to *receive* a taste in this world of the banquet that is to come. *Giving* life has always been a Family matter with God, involving no less than Father, Son and Holy Spirit. So has saving it.

Far more than saving, *God is Salvation*... beginning to end, period.

# *The Worshipping* (Noah)

No singular historical event substantiates the fact that man cannot save himself from the wrath of God due sin as does the World Flood (see Genesis 6:1-9:17). Cataclysmic and monumental, the unparalleled event marks a turning point in man's relationship with God, as well as in world development.

From the time of Adam to the days of Noah (the man chosen by God to ride out the Flood), mankind greatly multiplied, and so did the wickedness within him. During those ten generations (see Luke 3:36-38), depravity so intensified that violence became the norm, searing man's conscience to evil desire. Little was held in check; chaos abounded (see Genesis 6:5).

But evil would not have the final say in this or any world. Come Judgment Day at time's end, perfect justice will be dispensed by God, delivering final restoration that will set all things right (see Matthew 12:36). Evil will be *given* its due (see Revelation 19:20; 20:10-15; 21:8), as will good, for God is holy (see Psalms 99:9), and God is just (see 2 Thessalonians 1:6).

In the meantime, the Flood that engulfed the world has provided man with a glimpse of the final judgment's magnitude, *giving* long-range insight. Dispensing divinely meshed wrath and mercy, God proved His holy justice to be inescapable by human effort. Point blankly, the Flood declared the necessity of man's compliance with God in order to have any hope of survival. Short term, it also provided an immediate reality check and much needed relief from sin's compounding effects on the world.

Generally speaking, man tends to *give* preference to his physical nature over his spiritual being. Consequently, he is more often than not driven by the temporal instead of governed by the eternal. In the Garden of Eden, when man---a spirit being in touch with Spirit God---looked at the Tree of the Knowledge of Good and Evil and saw opportunity for self-advancement, he imagined that physical fruit could produce spiritual results. His topsy-turvy thinking led to the world's chaos. Had he seen the tree only in terms of opportunity to honor God with obedience to God's Word, recognizing that spirit is by far the greater, right order would have remained in the world. But in choosing forbidden fruit over reverence for God's Word, man submitted spirit to flesh---the greater to the lesser---in confounded thinking that confounded order. He made a mess.

The mess resulted when temptation disclosed that man had a lack of faith in God that was undermining their relationship without man's general awareness. But when man *accepted* temptation over God's Word in wrong thinking, his lack of faith rose to the surface and became evident for all to see and rightly acknowledge.

The time would come in history when Jesus would reveal that temptation need not be *accepted* by any man. Immediately following His baptism, Jesus would be led by the Spirit into the wilderness for forty days of fasting (see Luke 4:1-13). During that time, temptation would be present, but unsuccessful against Jesus, who would lean fully upon the Spirit's guidance in knowledge of God's Word to keep Him right with His Father. Jesus would reveal what men had yet to learn: "The Spirit gives life; the flesh counts for nothing" (John 6:63a).

Confident of His identity as the loved Son of God the Father (see Matthew 3:17; Mark 1:11; Luke 3:22), Jesus would not be threatened in the least by Satan's insinuating remarks that were designed to shift Jesus' focus from His Father onto Himself. Refusing to be led astray, Jesus would retain right focus by responding to Satan's words of temptation with His Father's words, not His own. Doing so would rightly honor His Father and avoid all attempts at self-promotion (see Hebrews 4:15).

To decline any specific temptation, however, only proves a man's faith in God in a particular place and time regarding a particular matter. Faith as a whole must be walked out over a lifetime of temptation. Only in its regular exercising is faith continually strengthened. As a man, Jesus would trust God each and every moment of His days on earth to defeat all worldly temptation.

No man other than Jesus, though, would ever be confronted by temptation to the degree that Jesus would be tempted on the evening of His impending arrest in the Garden of Gethsemane, a name meaning *oil press²* (see Luke 22:39-46). There, knowing the suffering of body and soul that were waiting for Him at the Cross, Jesus would proceed solely by faith. Unlike in the Garden of Eden, where man had *accepted* temptation to try to make himself a god, Jesus, who is God, would *reject* the temptation to allow His humanity to sin against God.

On His knees, Jesus would sweat blood, as He would seek the strength to remain in His Father's will. He would win the battle when, knowing the personal cost to Him, He would commit His death along with His life to His Father. Prayer would be the strengthening agent that would deliver resolution, *giving* the Spirit triumph over flesh and proving faith to be the highest form of worship.

> [Jesus], being in very nature God, did not consider equality with God something to be grasped, but made himself nothing, taking the very nature of a servant, being made in human likeness. And being found in appearance as a man, he humbled himself and became obedient to death---even death on a cross. (Philippians 2:6-8)

By serving the needs of all men according to His Father's will, Jesus' life and death would define worship. His humbleness would lead in the end to Jesus *receiving* the seat of highest honor at

---

2 ² James Strong, *Strong's Exhaustive Concordance of the Bible: Expanded Edition* (Peabody, MA: Hendrickson Publisher, 2007), s.v. "Gethsemane."

the Father's right hand (see Hebrews 1:3), for "he who humbles himself will be exalted" (Luke 14:11b).

A truly humble man dares judge no man for fear of self-incrimination (see Matthew 7:2). Instead, he serves all men in recognition of their equality before God (see Acts 10:34). Even Jesus, the only man capable of rightly judging another, would not judge.

> As for the person who hears my words but does not keep them, I do not judge him. For I did not come to judge the world, but to save it. There is a judge for the one who rejects me and does not accept my words; that very word which I spoke will condemn him at the last day. (John 12:47-48)

Judgment is coming, but not by Jesus. On Judgment Day, each man's *acceptance* or *rejection* of God's Word will judge him accordingly. A man's word will be his judge. Jesus---the Word of God---will serve all who will have *accepted* salvation in Him, for He will be their only defense from evil's condemnation. The rightness of Jesus' humbleness in serving God and man, even in crucifixion---the pinnacle of all humility, would be life-*giving* (see Philippians 2:8).

Just prior to sharing the Last Supper with His twelve closest disciples, right before His death, Jesus would stoop down to wash the dirt and grime from His disciples' feet to *give* them an idea of just how low He would be willing to go for their sakes (see John 13:1-17). This act that was typically reserved for the lowest household servants would be performed by Jesus on men who would have rather high regard for themselves in being included at

Jesus' Passover table. Relishing their importance in reclining there, these men, who would have been under His tutelage for more than three years by then, would still lack understanding of Jesus' purpose in being with them. But in the end, all who would steadfastly follow Jesus down one road after another to journey's end, humbly *accepting* direction from Jesus, would be *given* new direction that would *give* life in its respect for God by living in right service to others.

> A new command I give you: As I have loved you, so you must love one another. (John 13:34)

The love and service that signify right living would be forever intertwined by Jesus with faith in God as true worship. But back in the days of Noah, man's concept of right living was mostly self-defined by men who worshipped themselves more than God. An "every man for himself" mentality created an isolationism that benefitted no one. The Flood would be an antidote to man's misconception, dispelling the notion that prideful independence from God and others is man's path forward to a life worth living.

But despite the evil rebelliousness that covered God's good world, God Himself was still present, faithfully serving Creation by acting in man's best interest. Unchangeable (see Malachi 3:6), God is life's Constant. His consistent words and deeds uphold each other in supporting all life. Without any false pride to misguide Him, God does not seek man's approval for ego's sake. He simply does what is right---best. Neither selfish nor spiteful, He does not throw temper tantrums to get His way, for His way, the right way, always prevails. Nor does He err in momentary impulsiveness, for He is never caught off-guard. Rather, God is the epitome of meekness—*strength under control.* Countering every move of evil with divine wisdom, God cannot lose in any manner.

With that being the case, how then could a good and loving God, who knew that man would be corrupted by sin, ever have *given* man the opportunity to oppose Him in the first place? Why did God place the Tree of the Knowledge of Good and Evil in the Garden of Eden? Why did He create a place where temptation could lead to downfall?

Consider this: At one point in Jesus' ministry, a crowd of disciples following Jesus would infuriate Pharisees (strict adherers to the Law of Moses that would come to direct Jewish life) by loudly praising Jesus. At the Pharisees' insistence that Jesus should rebuke His disciples, Jesus would say, "... if they keep quiet, the stones will cry out" (Luke 19:40).

The stones rightly would do so, for all Creation glorifies God by existence. But remember that men, made in God's image, can purposefully acknowledge God's supremacy by choosing to enter into a higher form of more intimate worship of Him.

In the Garden of Eden, where man knew only God and God's full provision, man had no concept of lack. Even if he had appreciated his Garden life to some degree, he still would have missed knowing the true gratitude that comes only in comparative awareness of what it means to be without. Lacking nothing but lack, man didn't and couldn't fully appreciate all that he had. Even though his daily walk with God was itself a life of worship, man had little if any concept of worship's purpose, meaning or power.

Man only has two choices as to how he can respond to God, and those choices were represented in the Garden of Eden by the Tree of Life and the Tree of the Knowledge of Good and Evil. Man could either gratefully *accept* his life with God as being more than sufficient, or he could seek the ever elusive and nonexistent "more." Had he chosen the first option, he would have worshipped God with an ongoing decision to continue eating from every tree but the Tree of the Knowledge of Good and Evil.

But he didn't. In choosing to eat the fruit of the off-limit Tree, man engaged in self-worship. In *accepting* the temptation to help himself to "more," he lost the good life that he had and he gained knowledge of lack. Ironically, that put him in a better position to recognize and appreciate God's goodness from that point forward.

When God chose at Creation to differentiate man from other life by *giving* him an ability to be cognizant of God, He also chose to *give* him the free will to worship God or not. Man's intimate worship of God that is mutually beneficial, serving both God and man by drawing men closer to God, can only come by way of a free will decision to engage in right worship. Without the license to not worship God, man's worship would be without potential for increasing man's fellowship with God.

The Garden choice of Trees was a test—an opportunity for man's advancement in his relationship with God. It was not temptation. Satan tempts; God does not (see James 1:13). The distinction matters, for while a test intends to draw men closer to God, temptation intends to further separate man from God.

Tests, being knowledge based, are *given* only when success is possible. Temptation, on the other hand, contains an unknown factor that attempts to lure men into miscalculation and eventual failure. While the Garden choice came with a directive from God that empowered man to choose wisely without doubt, the Garden temptation came with a suggestion from Satan that created doubt. While "The Choice" was *given* in man's best interest, enabling him to grow in faith; "The Temptation" served only Satan by putting distance between God and man, fulfilling evil desire.

But if "The Choice" were indeed good and necessary, how could a good and loving God then flood the world that He so loved when man fell for temptation and failed the test? If God is "the builder of everything" (Hebrews 3:4b), how could He purposefully destroy?

The perceived destruction of the Flood was actually the destruction of the destruction that evil had delivered to the world. Similar to using a double negative in English grammar to produce a positive result, such destruction is constructive in nature. It is comparable to clearing away tornadic debris with a bulldozer to initiate the rebuilding process, allowing life to move forward.

Though Jesus would one day build life *in* death, life is not built *on* death.

The Flood was an act of God's good and loving precision in both its judgment and execution. Had God wanted to end life on the Earth, He would have done so. But He didn't; He was rebuilding life in its totality, not destroying it. While some men lost physical life in the Flood, mankind gained in the long run. The Flood *took* time away from sin's overriding destruction of the Earth and returned it to the promotion of salvation, helping to maximize the saving of souls.

Physical life is a gift from God that is to be honored and cherished as such, but not on the same scale as spiritual life. Made by a triune Spirit God (Father, Son and Holy Spirit), man also is a three part being. He has a spirit, a soul (mind, will and emotions) and a body (see 1 Thessalonians 5:23b).

Man's spirit and soul are everlasting, existing forever, either with God in heaven or without God in hell. But his body, in its current state, is a temporary container allowing him to inhabit this physical world for a limited time while choosing his future dwelling. At the moment of a man's physical death, his spirit and soul leave his body, living on. But his body, an empty shell void of life, decays, returning to dust (see Ecclesiastes 12:7).

The Flood's tough love that *took* physical life from some men was akin to amputating a gangrene limb to prevent death's spread, saving life. The Flood was not an instrument of death, but an instrument of deliverance, restoring right order in its triumph over evil.

Evil puts on a big show, feigning strength that it does not possess. Its deceptive front is like that of a movie set façade, making evil appear mightier than it is. But evil is no more powerful than a pretentious weakling who lifts fake dumbbells over his head to impress a crowd of onlookers. Once the deception is revealed, the crowd disperses to find something legitimate to admire. Likewise, evil's power is one of deceptive suggestion that Truth deflates. Evil's only power is in its ability to suggest, not enforce, defiance of God. Evil cannot make a man choose its ways over God's way.

Man's power of free will is far greater, for with it he can reject evil. Only when he submits to evil's temptation does he then empower evil by becoming its instrumentation, fulfilling its desires. Evil's suggestions, though having evil intent, are by themselves meaningless. Without man's cooperation, evil intentions amount to nothing.

True power belongs to God, the Source of all power, for power lies in Truth that overcomes all evil. Being Truth itself, God can neither be deceived in self-deception nor tempted by self-defiance. By revealing Himself in Truth to men, God strengthens them in their stand against temptation by *giving* them greater Truth to stand upon.

Prior to the Flood, God *gave* Noah knowledge that served God's good and loving purpose of sustaining human and animal life through the Flood. Choosing only one man, Noah, and that man's family, God offered the world a new beginning. He delivered a controlled cleansing of the Earth's surface while saving Noah's seed in continuation of mankind. The Flood foreshadowed the world's coming salvation through Jesus, whose blood would one day cleanse the world of all sin and enable men to experience spiritual rebirth. Both cleansings would provide men with hope, but of different calibers.

Noah wasn't Jesus by any stretch of the imagination. But, he was apparently as good as man came, for the Bible records that "Noah was a righteous man, blameless among the people of his time, and he walked with God" (Genesis 6:9). He walked with God...

A good God was still present, caring for man. As flood waters raged, covering the Earth, they rose only as high and lasted as long as God ordained necessary. Doing only good, no evil, God saved life while diminishing corruption. The experience put Noah right where every man should be: in a position of complete humility before God Almighty---the One whose Being commands the utmost, awesome and reverential respect reserved for Him alone.

> Fear God and keep his commandments, for this is the whole duty of man. For God will bring every deed into judgment, including every hidden thing, whether it is good or evil. (Ecclesiastes 12:13b-14)

Noah reverenced God even before the Flood. He spent untold years obediently adhering to God's instructions to build an enormous ark in the desert that would allow him to escape a coming flood that he didn't understand. That's faith (see Hebrews 11:7;

James 2:17). Noah sacrificed time and energy to do that which God had said would ultimately benefit both Noah and his family. Even though doing so was undoubtedly life-interrupting and inconvenient, not to mention hard work, Noah honored God with obedience that benefitted life.

But after the Flood, Noah's worship of God *took* a decidedly upward turn to lead him into a different kind of worship, one that was offered in greater knowledge and understanding of both God and himself. In the ark, Noah had tasted both God's supreme power and His exorbitant mercy. Neither one was wasted on Noah, who had been spared from a fate that "could have, would have and should have" been his, had God not selected him to be saved by grace through faith.

As soon as Noah again had firm ground under his feet, he immediately built an altar and worshipped God. So pleased was God that He promised to never again curse the ground because of the evil that was in men's hearts. *The righteous worship of a single man changed the world for the betterment of all mankind.*

One man was all God had needed to reveal the Truth that delivered God's intended restoration for the world at that particular time. More Truth and restoration would follow, in time's due course, according to God's divine wisdom that would continue working in mankind's best interest.

So, as God had once blessed Adam in the Garden of Eden (see Genesis 5:2), God so blessed Noah and Noah's sons in their new world, saying, "Be fruitful and increase in number and fill the earth"

(Genesis 9:1b). But beyond blessing, God made covenant with all life on the Earth, vowing mercifully never again to use a world flood to cut off all life.

So life went on. Noah planted a vineyard and later harvested a wine that was to his liking. All seemed good, until Ham, one of Noah's sons, dishonored his father when opportunity tempted him to do so. Then, learning later of Ham's disloyalty to him, Noah cursed Canaan, Ham's son, so that Ham too would experience shame from his son.

Canaan's descendants would be the ones who would toil and work the land that would become God's Promised Land. They would build and add to the land's blessings of riches (see Deuteronomy 6:10-12), only to have God then *give* the land to the Israelites---God's chosen people through whom Jesus would eventually be born. The Israelites would come from Shem, one of Noah's two sons who had treated Noah with respect when Ham had shamed him. The Israelites would become God's nation of choice: the Jewish nation of Israel, through whom God would deliver salvation to the world (see John 4:22).

Every act of both good and evil is woven by God Almighty into His salvation plan for the benefit of all mankind. God is too big---too perfect---to be circumvented, and all men will know so. The day is coming soon, relatively speaking, when all men will bow, as all knees will bend (see Isaiah 45:23; Romans 14:11; Philippians 2:10), worshipping God reverently in exaltation of His supremacy (see Romans 12:1).

For he has set a day when he will judge the world with justice by the man he has appointed. (Acts 17:31a)

That Man, through whom justice will be dispensed, is God's One and Only Son: Jesus. Jesus would envelop right living in a life of service to others, while admonishing all men to live likewise, saying, "Be merciful just as your Father is merciful" (Luke 6:36).

In the eternal moment when due justice occurs, comprehension of the magnitude of God's mercy in the gift of salvation will strike each man like an overwhelming flood. Each man who is saved will know with certainty that without God's mercy, his fate "could have, would have and should have" gone another direction. God's love for man and God's hatred of evil will be evident as never before, witnessed in the mercy of God in Christ Jesus that will separate the two.

> At one time, we too were foolish, disobedient, deceived and enslaved by all kinds of passions and pleasures. We lived in malice and envy, being hated and hating one another. But when the kindness and love of God our Savior appeared, he saved us, not because of righteous things we had done, but because of his mercy. He saved us through the washing of rebirth ... (Titus 3:3-5a)

To love all that is good demands actively participating in eliminating evil, for evil is a constriction that attempts to impede the flow of God's loving-goodness throughout Creation. It also demands *giving* every advantage to the growth of all that is good through the grace of love's merciful second chances that don't stop at two... or even at seventy-seven (see Matthew 18:21-22), but are endless.

Because of the LORD's great love we are not consumed, for his compassions never fail. They are new every morning; ... (Lamentations 3:22-23a)

Far more than merciful, *God is Mercy*... beginning to end, period.

# *The Turning* (Abraham)

As world population increased following the Flood, man moved into new territory, in more ways than one (see Genesis 10). While spreading out geographically, he found it advantageous to begin congregating in communities for mutual benefit. Sharing one common language enabled him to pool thoughts and abilities to produce feats by combined efforts that would have been difficult, if not impossible, to accomplish alone.

But as beneficial as cooperation was, greater harm than good came from its misuse. The more man was drawn to man, the less he was drawn to God. As mankind placed greater emphasis on personal abilities, pride became a greater tripping hazard. For man's own good, as well as for that of the world, man's admiration needed to be shifted---turned---from self to God.

On the Plain of Shinar, where a city was being built, man instigated a plan to make man's name great---equal to that of God (see Genesis 11:1-9). Using man-made bricks instead of stones, men began erecting a tower that would be self-honoring. The tower would literally and figuratively lift man to new heights of grandeur, proving him capable of doing whatever he so pleased to do. It fostered the same wrong thinking that had led to man's downfall.

But God, knowing man's heart (see Acts 1:24), looked down upon the scene, realizing the detrimental effects that such collaboration apart from God would have on man. Between man's perceived self-righteousness and his self-acclamation, he would never see a need to turn to God. Though man was proud of himself at that moment, his future was at stake.

For his own good, man needed to be diverted from vain aspirations. He needed something that would complicate his efforts, confusing the matter in a manner that would reflect his limitations. God's solution to the problem was phenomenally simple. He diversified man's speech, creating languages that sounded like nonsensical babel to one another. When man lost comprehension of one another's words, he also lost the ability to assimilate one another's concepts into cohesive action. Frustrated, man scattered in thought and action, completing step one of the turning.

The language barrier, however, would not last forever. The day would come following the resurrection and ascension of Jesus when men from various nations would once again be reunited through a common language. But the language would be a God-given one from the Holy Spirit, one that is beyond man's natural ability to produce or comprehend. In receiving the Holy Spirit, Jesus' first disciples (followers who would accept Jesus as Lord and Savior) would be the first through whom the Spirit's utterance of the new language would flow. Their anointed language would be heard by others, drawing men together in greater understanding of God through the sharing of the Good News of Jesus Christ. By

Holy Spirit power within them, men would become likeminded---One in Spirit with God and one another. God, not man, would be glorified in the building that He would do through the lives of men (see Acts 1:4-5, 2:1-47).

But long before that day could arrive, God would first begin the reunification process by choosing a man---just one---who would be willing to turn from worldly ways to walk with Him. As Satan had once used the disobedience of the one man, Adam, to accomplish evil through doubt, God would repeatedly choose to use the obedience of one man at a time to accomplish His good and perfect will (see Romans 12:2) through faith.

The man to be chosen at this time was Abram, whose name God changed to Abraham. His new name, meaning "father of many" (Genesis 17:4-5), reflected his new covenant identity with God. It was one of friendship (see 2 Chronicles 20:7; Isaiah 41:8; James 2:23) that was built on Abraham's faith in both God and God's words of promise that were *given* to him (see Roman 4:17).

So, as Noah had once been deemed by God to be righteous (see Genesis 6:9b), so too was Abraham also deemed by God to be righteous (see Genesis 15:6). However great Abraham's initial faith in God may or may not have been when God first called Abraham to leave home and family, it was sufficient to cause him to pack up and move. When God said that it was time to go, Abraham followed God's lead. As he went, his relationship with God deepened and faith grew, proving itself to be sufficient as needed in each successive leg of the journey.

The faith that God developed in Abraham met Abraham's need for God and God's reasons for having selected Abraham. Abraham's faith *gave* him expectation that the promises that God had *given* to him would indeed all be fulfilled. That included the promise that God would birth a son to him through whom God would birth a nation (see Genesis 12, 15).

God's promise of parenthood to Abraham and his wife, Sarah, sounded absurd, considering their ages and physical conditions, for Abraham was one hundred, and Sarah was ninety (see Genesis 17:17). "Yet [Abraham] did not waver through unbelief regarding the promise of God, but was strengthened in his faith and gave glory to God, being fully persuaded that God had power to do what he had promised" (Romans 4:20-21).

Fulfilment came by the power of God working in Abraham and Sarah to produce a son, Isaac—a manifestation of God's faithfulness, increasing Abraham's faith all the more (see Genesis 21:1-7). When the time came, years later, for God to prove the strength of Abraham's faith by asking Abraham to sacrifice Isaac on an altar, Abraham's heart and mind were fully prepared by God to pass the test (see Genesis 22:1-19).

The heart-rending story, foreshadowing God the Father's sacrificing of Jesus on the Cross, is one that must be reckoned by each man's faith in God. The question arises as to how any man could do what God asked of Abraham. The answer lies in Abraham's faith. Abraham had every expectation of God restoring Isaac's life after the sacrifice in order to fulfill God's promise that a nation would come through his son, who as of then did not yet have a child. Abraham fully expected Isaac to return home alive with him that evening (see Genesis 22:5).

The conundrum to men is that "... while we were still sinners, Christ died for us" (Romans 5:8). How could God ever have desired to sacrifice His own righteous Son to save unrighteous man? How could a good and loving God have been pleased with the outlandish crucifixion of His own Son, crushing Him for man's sake (see Isaiah 53:10)?

Though God knew, of course, that Jesus would be raised from death to eternal life, that doesn't explain His pleasure in His Son's suffering. The answer, contemplated in countless books designated to that singular consideration alone, lies far beyond man's grasp to completely understand, for perfect righteousness is incomprehensible by men who are used to thinking in unrighteous terms.

But the answer boils down to this: It was the right thing to do, so God did it. That's it, pure and simple. God saved man because He could, and He did so via His own life in the Son (see John 6:57) because it was the best way to fulfill all that needed to be fulfilled in creating perfect unity between God and men.

God did His part, laying out salvation's plan of action and choosing the men who would rightly fulfill it. Abraham did his part, as all men can do theirs, simply by trusting God in following God's direction. As with Noah, it wasn't Abraham's performance that made him righteous in God's eyes, but his faith in God that did.

Abraham trusted God to fulfill His Word, to completely fulfill His every Word, no matter how absurd or impossible it sounded.

So by faith, Abraham followed God to a new homeland that Abraham's descendants would one day *receive* from God through inheritance of the promise that God had made to Abraham. That promise would be confirmed by God, first to Isaac (see Genesis 26:2-5) and then to Isaac's son, Jacob (see Genesis 28:10-15). Passed from generation to generation, the promise would live in the family's thoughts and words, until it would finally come to pass more than four hundred years into the future, exactly as God had first promised Abraham (see Genesis 15:13).

During those four hundred plus years, faith was needed by the generations who awaited the promise's manifestation. The fulfillment that could not yet be seen had to be believed by faith with expectant hope until it would be seen, for "... faith is being sure of what we hope for and certain of what we do not see" (Hebrews 11:1). Though unseen Himself, God was ever-present in the interim, blessing all who were awaiting the promise's fulfillment by turning the family's difficulties into advantages that would fulfill His purposes in designing the wait.

First, Isaac had his problems. He married Rebekah, a woman from his father's family (see Genesis 24), only to later purposefully put her in harm's way, as his father had once done to his mother for personal self-benefit (see Genesis 26:7-11). Then, finding his father's wells filled in by others, he had to dig them out again to supply his flocks with the water that they needed to live (see Genesis 26:18).

After a time of childlessness, Isaac prayed to God, who then *gave* Isaac and Rebekah twin sons (see Genesis 25:21-26). But Isaac favored the first-born, Esau, and Rebekah favored Jacob, the younger, dividing the family's loyalties (see Genesis 25:28). Esau grew to wrongly despise his birthright as the family's eldest son and purposefully forfeited it to Jacob for a mere bowl of stew to satisfy his disdain (see Genesis 25:29-34). Jacob, on the other hand, *took* Esau's rightful blessing by intentionally deceiving Isaac in a plot masterminded by Rebekah in order to usurp his brother's rights (see Genesis 27).

Without birthright or blessing, Esau then married idol worshipping Hittite women, dismaying his parents (see Genesis 26:34-35) and setting the stage for future animosity between his descendants and the God-worshipping descendants of Jacob. Jacob feared Esau's anger against him for his ruse against Isaac. So with his father's blessing, he fled to the land of his mother's family, distancing himself from his brother (see Genesis 27:41-28:5). There Jacob *received* the wife, Rachel, he desired, plus several others through trickery employed against him by his uncle, Rachel's father. In turn, Jacob amassed a wealth of sheep from his uncle through trickery of his own (see Genesis 29-30).

The family that God was building was full of deceit and disappointment, as was the world at large. But the family's lack of forthright honesty with one another did not stop God from blessing them in order to accomplish His good purpose. So the family was blessed, not because they were good (they weren't), but because God is.

But not even Jacob's abundant blessings could lift the burden of guilt and fear that he carried with him from his disloyalty to his brother. So when the time came for Jacob to return home, he made the journey in trepidation, fearing his brother's revenge. Only when Jacob finally humbled himself face-to-face with Esau to seek his brother's mercy did his decision to do right offer him relief. Though Esau, who had been blessed by God with his own abundance, declined Jacob's offer of restitution for the wrong that Jacob had done to him, Esau *gave* Jacob the gift that would make true restoration between them possible. Jacob *received* his brother's complete forgiveness (see Genesis 33:1-17).

Unqualified forgiveness would be stressed repeatedly by God in various ways throughout time's continuum as being necessary for right relationships. Man, though, would repeatedly struggle against the personal humility that is required in seeking and *receiving* another's forgiveness, as well as in freely *giving* it as needed. Man's pride would continue pitting his ego against God's righteousness in a futile battle of wrong against right that would keep men distanced from God and one another.

Jacob's personal struggle with God over the matter *took* a decisive turn the night before Jacob reunited with Esau, *giving* Jacob the courage to do what was right. The struggle was not easy. But wrestling throughout the night, he persevered to a life-altering conclusion that lifted his relationships with God and men to new levels. By morning, Jacob had a new identity that was reflected in his new name: Israel (see Genesis 32:22-32). The name would be shared with his family and the nation that God was building through them, for they too would also have to persevere through ongoing struggles with God.

The promise that God had *given* to Abraham was also ongoing. It continued passing by inheritance from Jacob/Israel to his twelve sons and then to their descendants, who would become the twelve tribes of Israel. Joseph---the first of Jacob's sons by Rachel---was Jacob's favorite and the one used by God to lead the family through their next difficult time. The forgiveness and blessings that had been *given* to Jacob were not wasted on him, but cultivated through him. The day would come when his sons would learn the benefits of forgiveness firsthand. Blessings would come to bear in the midst of misgivings that, though meant for harm, would be used by God for the good of the world in the family's reunification.

The family's problem was one of pride. It came to a head when Joseph's jealous brothers, tired of hearing about Joseph's prideful dreams, wanted to kill him outright, due to pride of their own (see Genesis 37). But Reuben, the oldest, convinced his brothers to drop Joseph into a cistern instead, keeping their hands, if not their hearts, free from bloodshed. There, Joseph would have been left to die had not the serendipitous passing of slave traders prompted Judah (Jacob's son through whom Jesus' earthly lineage would flow) to suggest selling Joseph instead.

Sold for twenty pieces of silver, Joseph was *taken* to Egypt against his will, while his brothers headed home to grieve their father with a deception that led him to believe that his beloved Joseph was dead. For momentary satisfaction, Joseph's brothers turned against God and family, burdening themselves with years of fearful guilt and shame.

In Egypt, Joseph's identity digressed from son to slave to prisoner (see Genesis 39-40). But the favor of God remained on Joseph, as God sustained him through thirteen years of unjust suffering. During his trials, Joseph never turned on God. Instead his faith matured in its testing and was *given* opportunity to shine when Joseph was raised by God out of his imprisonment to be made second in command over all of Egypt (see Genesis 41:40). In one moment of time, Joseph *received* power and authority with which he could bless others, if he would choose to rightly do so, and he did (see Genesis 41:46-57).

No opportunity *given* to Joseph to bless others would be any more golden than the one of restoring his father's family. Twice, once after his brothers first arrived in Egypt and again after they moved their entire family to Egypt, Joseph dispelled his brothers' fear of vengeance by rightly choosing to earnestly assure them that he had indeed forgiven all (see Genesis 45, 50).

> Joseph said to them, "Don't be afraid. Am I in the place of God? You intended to harm me, but God intended it for good to accomplish what is now being done, the saving of many lives. So then, don't be afraid. I will provide for you

and your children." And he reassured them and spoke kindly to them. (Genesis 50:19-21)

The family's reunion foreshadowed the reconciliation of God's Family through the forgiveness of sin that would be *given* in its time by the blood of Jesus. Relationships broken by sin would *receive* complete restoration only through forgiveness. Nailed to the Cross, Jesus Himself would pray, "Father, forgive them, for they do not know what they are doing" (Luke 23:34).

For thirty silver coins (see Matthew 26:15)---the value placed upon a slave (see Exodus 21:32; Zechariah 11:12), Judas Iscariot, one of Jesus' twelve hand-picked disciples, would betray Jesus into death. But in the end, every loved disciple would abandon Jesus. Peter, one of His three closest friends, would deny any association with Jesus for the price of self-protection. The others would all run for their lives during Jesus' arrest for the same reason (see Mark 14:50). Each one would remain hidden or quiet with greater concern for self than Jesus.

Yet Jesus would allow Himself to be bound and led (see Matthew 27:2) into a one-of-a-kind separation from His Father for the sake of all men, whose disloyalty to God would be placed upon Him in the best interest of all. Freely forgiving all men all sin, Jesus would turn men's deadly pride upon itself to leave men humbly dwarfed before God. Reunion of men and God would *give* Jesus reason to look beyond the scourging and Crucifixion to rejoice in His opportunity to set His Father's world right (see Hebrews 12:2).

Being both God and man, Jesus would bring His Father and His brothers---those reborn into God's Family in Him---to Oneness. From "far above all rule and authority, power and dominion, and every name that is invoked, not only in the present age, but also in the one to come" (Ephesians 1:21), Jesus would unite Family forever.

> All this is from God, who reconciled us to himself through Christ and gave us the ministry of reconciliation: that God was reconciling the world to himself in Christ, not counting men's sins against them. And he has committed to us the message of reconciliation. We are therefore Christ's ambassadors, as though God were making his appeal through us. We implore you on Christ's behalf: Be reconciled to God. God made him who had no sin to be sin for us, so that in him we might become the righteousness of God. (2 Corinthians 5:18-21)

Far more than reconciling, *God is Reconciliation*... beginning to end, period.

# *The Increasing* (Moses)

On their way into Egypt to live with Joseph, Jacob's descendants---worshippers of the God of Abraham, Isaac and Jacob---numbered seventy. The number that was seemingly large for a family was still small for the nation that God had promised. According to God's promise to Abraham, the family would yet become a nation with a home of its own, a nation through whom the world would be blessed, the nation through whom God would reveal Himself to the world, *giving* salvation.

With purposeful intent, God would continue growing His Family-nation into one of world renowned stature and faith, one that would make a Name for God on earth that would be rightly respected above all other names. God's work in the lives of His Family-nation would lead them to know to whom they belonged and on whom life depends. God would build faith in Him that would never doubt Him.

The growth process would necessitate men learning to put God first---before and above all else, *giving* God thanks and praise at all times and in all circumstances (see Colossians 3:17). God's strength, not theirs, would uphold them. Though they would fail many times, God never would.

When Jacob's family crossed into Egypt, they were still in their infancy as a nation. They needed time and proper nurturing to grow strong, to be made by God into a formidable and unconquerable opponent of idol worshippers everywhere.

Growth (building up, increasing) is fundamental in God's Creation. Sowing, tending and harvesting life-giving crops of every kind is initiated and accomplished by God, who produces greater reflections of His Being in all that He nurtures. In life, growth is imperative. Without growth, stagnation leads to varying degrees of death. Even "Jesus grew in wisdom and stature, and in favor with God and men" (Luke 2:52).

A day would come in Jesus' earthly ministry when He would tell a parable describing the Word of God as being like a seed that is planted in the hearts of men. He would explain that the Word's ability to take root and grow, producing a harvest, depends upon both the condition of the heart (soil) that *receives* the Word (seed) and upon how well the planting is tended. The harvest produced in a man's life would reveal much about a man (see Matthew 13:1-23; Mark4:3-20; Luke 8:4-15).

Jesus would also describe the Kingdom of God in terms of growth. Again, He would use a parable about seeds to explain it.

> "This is what the Kingdom of God is like: A man scatters seed on the ground. Night and day, whether he sleeps or gets up, the seed sprouts and grows, though he does not know how. All by itself, the soil produces grain---first the stalk, then the head, then the full kernel in the head. As soon as the grain is ripe, he puts the sickle to it, because the harvest has come" (Mark 4:26-29; see also Ezekiel 17:22-24).

Growth is indicative that a harvest is coming, and Jacob's growing family was a sign that the promise of God that had been made to Abraham was in production. In only three generations, God had grown the family of seventy from the seed of one. But even at that, as they moved into Egypt, the family of Hebrews—their name as of that time that refers to Abraham's ancestral line from Eber (see Genesis 11:16)—still had a lot of growing to do.

To God's self-sustained glory, the family would continue growing in good times and bad, even during widespread famine that first prompted Joseph's brothers to go to Egypt. There they found Joseph providing sustenance to many who were in great need. In that time and place, Joseph had been prepared by God with knowledge and wisdom that enabled people from many lands to be fed through his enlightenment. By God's planting of Joseph in Egypt to oversee food distribution before the famine arose, God prepared to meet the needs of many, especially those of His growing Family-nation (see Genesis 47:13-27).

Through Joseph's God-*given* favor with Pharaoh (Egypt's head ruler), the family was *given* refuge in Goshen, a land within Egypt that God had prepared as their temporary dwelling place. There they shepherded their flocks in a lifestyle and livelihood that Egyptians found detestable (see Genesis 46:31-34). So even while they were residing in Egypt, they were set apart from Egyptians.

For a time, the family lived well in Egypt (see Genesis 47:27). Then came a time when a Pharaoh, who did not know of Joseph, came into power. At that time, idol worshipping Egyptians developed a growing resentment of foreign Hebrews and their foreign God. Fearing an imagined Hebrew revolt, the Egyptians submitted to the evil that they cultivated within their own wrong thinking. Disregarding the Hebrews' basic human rights and dignity, the Egyptians utilized harsh taskmasters to violently oppress the Hebrews into doing as they demanded. They forced Hebrews to be subservient to Egyptian will (see Exodus 1:8-11).

Evil is ever-present in this world. It doesn't *take* sabbaticals, but rather does lay low at times to await opportunity to present itself anew. Even in Satan's unsuccessful temptation of Jesus that would one day occur in the wilderness, Satan's prideful thinking would be such that, after failing, he would simply decide to wait for a more "opportune time" (Luke 4:13).

More than three years later, Satan would come to spot the opportunity for which he had been waiting. It would be present in the person of Judas Iscariot, Jesus' disciple, who would be willing to lead officials to Jesus in order for them to arrest Him. Entering Judas (see Luke 22:3), Satan would then watch "for an opportunity to hand Jesus over to [chief priests and the officers of the temple guard] when no crowd was present" (Luke 22:6).

Satan is ever working to bring down (decrease, reduce, lessen) the Kingdom that God is building. So when Satan would not be able to defeat Jesus directly through temptation, he would simply reroute his efforts through a more cooperative individual. Similarly, the Egyptians' cooperation with evil in oppressing the Hebrews was a secondary route employed by Satan to reduce the Hebrew family's faith in God by means of relentless mistreatment. If Satan couldn't stop them from believing in God, then he would work on getting them to at least question God's faithful loving-goodness towards them.

Ironically, though, by oppressing the Hebrews, the Egyptians unwittingly enslaved themselves to the evil with which they had sided. Choosing to use their God-*given* lives to oppress the lives of others, all for imagined personal gain, would lead the Egyptians in the end to nothing but their own loss. The more the Egyptians beat the Hebrews down, the more God built them up (see Exodus 1:12). God couldn't lose, and, attempting to live apart from God, the Egyptians couldn't win.

Even during times of increasing hardship, Jacob's descendants continued growing in number by the favor that God *gave* them in childbearing (see Exodus 1:15-21). Confined within Egypt, they experienced little outside infiltration, so that, despite any idol worship that may have slipped in among them or foreigners who may have joined their ranks, the faith of Abraham, Isaac and Jacob multiplied along with the family's increasing growth rate.

Throughout the family's four hundred year stay in Egypt, they thrived continually, independent of treatment. By the time that their promised deliverance from Egypt would arrive, the family that had entered as seventy would emerge as an Israelite nation of possibly two million people strong: more than 600,000 men, who were twenty years of age or older and capable of fighting, plus the women and children (see Numbers 1:46).

Endurance was behind their thriving. Had the Hebrews been released from Egypt before the appointed time, the potential for good that God would come to accomplish through their growth would not have been fully realized, and evil would have been effective in having its way. The oppression had to be endured until the Hebrews had achieved sufficient strengthening from God to meet the challenges of the times ahead. While God was growing the family, Satan was doing his best, unsuccessfully, to stifle their growth.

Interestingly, the extended stay of Jacob's family in Egypt offered the Egyptians potential good. The Egyptians had plenty of God-*given* opportunity to come to know and worship the One True God through the believing Hebrews living in their land. But they didn't. Just prior to the Hebrews' eventual deliverance from Egypt, the words of the Pharaoh of that time would reveal the Egyptians' disregard for the Hebrews' God.

> Pharaoh said, "Who is the LORD that I should obey him and let Israel go? I do not know the LORD and I will not let Israel go." (Exodus 5:2)

Pharaoh's words would indicate an attitude of pride that persisted during the four centuries that the Hebrews and Egyptians lived side-by-side. In the end, Egyptian perseverance in worshipping idols instead of God would be the means to the Hebrews achieving the strength necessary to walk with God out of their oppression by first having walked with Him through it (see Romans 5:3-4). Strength would be advantage.

Despite any appearances that may have seemed to indicate otherwise to the waiting Hebrews, God and time were both on their side. Proof would come in deliverance. The Hebrews wouldn't need to fight their oppressors in order to gain their freedom. Instead, God would fight for them. They would only need to continue crying out to God for His much needed help (see Exodus 2:23-25). The only cost to them would be the humility that they would show in faithfully asking God, not idols, to save them. On the other hand, prideful Egyptian idol-worship would prove more expensive than the Egyptians ever imagined, costing them both worldly valuables (see Exodus 12:35-36) and Egyptian lives (see Exodus 14:26-28).

Oppression is never God's desire for anyone. Rather, it develops from beliefs that are out of synch with the Truth of God. While oppression is most often thought of in physical terms, it is derived from wrong thinking. When the Hebrews would eventually be delivered out of Egypt, they would leave physical oppression behind. But they would still carry oppression with them in the form of a slave mentality that would continue to wrongly berate them.

Their *acceptance* of self-imposed limitations in the midst of newly acquired freedom would spring from lifelong mandatory compliance to demeaning Egyptian mistreatment. Oppression would survive in memory long after freedom's arrival. The belittling comments and derogatory treatment of years gone by, firmly etched in their hearts and minds, would continue projecting an impression of mistaken identity and devalued worth that would cheat the Israelites out of *receiving* the full benefit of their God-*given* freedom. Self-imposed bondage would be metaphorically akin to lugging around a ball and chain to which they were not attached. They were free to set it down at any time and move on without it.

But to do so, they would need someone whose understanding of freedom would be far greater than their own. The One Man who would have the understanding to lead all men in total freedom would be Jesus Christ. The day would come when Jesus, in beginning His ministry, would read from the scroll of Isaiah to declare, in essence, that freedom for prisoners and release from oppression are worth dying for (see Luke 4:18). Later, God would affirm freedom's importance through Paul, an apostle of Jesus Christ, saying, "It is for freedom that Christ has set us free" (Galatians 5:1a).

Long before that day would arrive, however, God first had to lead the Israelites out of Egyptian oppression, using a man of His choosing to do so. That man was to be Moses. Singled out by God before birth for this particular leadership position (see Ephesians 2:10), Moses was *given* a life that differed from other Hebrews in Egypt. By his mother's God-*given* courageous wisdom and by his God-*given* favor with Pharaoh's daughter, Moses was raised knowing abundance (see Exodus 2:1-10). He also knew a freedom that enabled him to come and go at will among the rich and the poor, the free and the oppressed.

As Moses grew, his expectations that privilege alone carries also would have grown along with him. While other Hebrew in Egypt were *receiving* orders from Egyptians, Moses' palace life undoubtedly *gave* him opportunity to *give* orders to Egyptians, *giving* him experience that was unknown to the others. But, equally important, Moses also knew his roots---his heritage, *giving* him an affinity for the people whom he would one day lead (see Hebrews 11:24-25).

But despite the opportunity that Moses was *given* to learn and grow in a prestigious environment, Moses' readiness to lead would not be complete without him *receiving* some necessary fieldwork. As a young adult, an irate Moses was guilty of having acted as judge, jury and executioner of an Egyptian, whom he had seen beating a Hebrew. In *taking* the Egyptian's life, Moses had done wrong in his attempt to do right (see Exodus 2:11-15).

Although Moses displayed a desire for justice and an intolerance for wrong, his actions also revealed a passion that needed to be tempered with control in order to be beneficial. Moses needed to grow in humbleness---deference to God's higher authority that would lead Moses to do God's will, God's way. The humbleness that Moses needed was *given* to him during Moses' self-exile to Midian that followed his murder of the Egyptian. There Moses *received* exactly what he needed:  forty years of shepherding experience (see Acts 7:30).

Moses had been raised with Egyptians, who detested shepherds, and above his people, who were shepherds. Shepherding *gave* Moses opportunity to better realize his roots and internalize his identity. Good shepherding also required commitment and self-sacrifice that Moses needed to learn by practicing on sheep before being entrusted with people.

Moses' shepherding years were a necessary realignment period that maximized the time's potential benefit for the world's highest good. The exile was not punishment, but opportunity for learning in a safe environment (see Exodus 4:19). By the time God had Moses sufficiently strengthened to lead the journey ahead, He had the Hebrew people in Egypt sufficiently strengthened to go with Moses. So God returned Moses to Egypt in a way that symbolized the change that God had produced in him. God returned Moses to Egypt humbly, with his family riding on a donkey (see Exodus 4:20).

A specified day in time would come when Jesus would enter Jerusalem humbly on a donkey amid the acclaim of cheering crowds (see John 12:12-19). But shortly thereafter, the cheers would change to jeers and the crowd around Jesus would become a lynch mob that would be out to hang him. The hanging would occur on a cross, and the humbleness of Jesus in hanging there would be unprecedented. Man's only rightful boast throughout eternity would be his boast in his Savior, Jesus (see 2 Corinthians 10:17), who would never boast about Himself. Though Jesus would have every reason by men's accounting to be proud, He would *receive* complete satisfaction in serving His Father in unconditional humility, exalting only His Father before all.

From worldly perspective, Moses too had reason, though to a much lesser degree, to be proud when he returned to Egypt. First, he had conversed with God in a God-initiated conversation (see Exodus 3:1-4:17) in which he had *received* a God-*given* career (see Exodus 3:10). He had also *received* a God-*given* Hebrew wife (see Genesis 25:1-6 for her Midianite roots) and two sons (see Exodus 2:21-22). Yet, in all this, God made Moses "more humble than anyone else on the face of the earth" (Numbers 12:3).

Moses' job of leading the Hebrews, who were known by then as Israelites, in their exodus from Egypt, was so extraordinary that it required a man of extraordinary humility---deference to God. It also required extraordinary measures and extraordinary preparation. The job commenced officially the moment when Moses turned from worldly concerns while shepherding sheep to pay heed to the supernatural:  a bush that was burning but not being consumed. By both noting and responding to the event, Moses met the God of his fathers---the God of Abraham, Isaac and Jacob---head-on at God's invitation, making God the God of Moses, as well (see Exodus 3:1-6). When God introduced Himself to Moses as "I AM WHO I AM" (Exodus 3:14), man's relationship with God changed forever.

From that time on, God led Moses, who was led to lead the Israelites out of Egypt and through the wilderness to their promised land. Once the exodus would begin, there would be no turning back. Miracles needed to accomplish God's will and meet the Israelites' needs would be deployed by God through Moses, who would need to respond obediently to God's words without hesitation. Likewise, the Israelites would also need to respond obediently to the words from God that Moses would relay to them. The Israelites would need to believe that God was for them, *giving* them good instruction through Moses for their benefit.

So God provided opportunity for the Israelites to develop faith in both God and Moses through God's use of the plagues that He delivered upon Egypt. The plagues did double duty, also serving to convince the Egyptians of the same two things: God was for the Israelites, and He was speaking through Moses.

Ten times, Moses was sent by God to Pharaoh to *give* Pharaoh a choice. Pharaoh could either allow the Israelites to leave Egypt, according to God's will, or he could *accept* a specified plague upon his nation. Each time, Pharaoh, who spoke for all Egyptians whether they agreed with him or not (see Exodus 9:20-21), chose to oppose God and *take* a plague (see Exodus 7:14-11:10). Each plague had an intended purpose of bringing about Egyptian repentance that would lead to Pharaoh's obedience in allowing the Israelites to leave Egypt. But each noncompliance of Pharaoh necessitated that each successive plague be of greater consequence than the previous one in order to yet bring about right repentance.

Repentance involves a realization that a departure from the will of God has occurred. It includes remorse. But even more, it is a decision to submit to God's correction, to purposefully be led by God back into alignment with Him. It is the act of turning from going one's own way to going God's way, acknowledging God as rightful Lord of all.

Even though the severity of the plagues continued increasing, Pharaoh stubbornly refused to humble himself to God's will. By steeling his mind, he hardened his heart to God and affirmed his own personal lack of God-like qualities. Though the plagues were negative in terms of their effects upon the Egyptians, they were good in that they revealed Truth, differentiating the power and authority that is God's alone from that which men *give* to one another. Simply stated, the plagues separated the proud from the humble in terms of men's positioning, relative to that of God, setting order right.

Pharaoh's pride was far more expensive than he ever anticipated. Only after his own son's death during the tenth plague did Pharaoh suffer sufficient remorse to cause him to momentarily comply with God and allow the Israelites to go. But since his decision was remorse driven instead of repentance driven, it was short lived. No sooner were the Israelites out of Egypt then Pharaoh reneged and went after them with his full army, intending to return them to Egyptian jurisdiction. His prideful wrong thinking caused Pharaoh to make a huge miscalculation that led his entire army to their deaths (see Exodus 14).

Though Pharaoh never benefited from the plagues, as he could have done, the Israelites did. The plagues greatly increased the Israelites' *acceptance* of Moses as being God's chosen leader and God's words of instruction as being for their benefit. Through the

Israelites' eye witness of the plagues that came upon Egypt, the Israelites grew to believe that God was for them, not against them, and that God had the necessary power to protect them from evil. Through Pharaoh's free will decisions to do wrong instead of right, God developed right trust of God in the Israelites that made them willing to follow Him by following Moses.

By the time Moses announced that a coming tenth plague would deliver death to every firstborn in Egypt, the Israelites willingly heeded Moses' instructions to the letter in order to preserve their lives. Sacrificing many lambs that day, they used the animals' blood to keep the death angel from *taking* the lives of Israelite men and livestock that night, as God had rightly forewarned would otherwise occur (see Exodus 11-12).

In years to come, this event known as Passover would be celebrated annually in a feast of thankful remembrance. It would serve to remind the Israelite nation that God was for them, not against them. Eventually the celebration would come to be held in Jerusalem, where in one particular year, the blood of countless sacrificed lambs would be trumped by the Blood of Jesus---the unblemished Lamb of God (see Hebrews 9:14; John 1:29). By God's will, Jesus would be "led like a lamb to the slaughter" (Isaiah 53:7b) to shed His blood to protect men from an otherwise certain death.

Much more than Moses or any other man could ever contemplate being, Jesus would be God's Good Shepherd, as well as God's Lamb. Jesus would describe Himself as such, stating the extent to which his good care of men would go.

I am the good shepherd. The good shepherd lays down his life for the sheep. (John 10:11)

A good shepherd is one who lives with his sheep day and night, watching over them fulltime. He *gives* priority to their wellbeing, not his, as he provides for their every need. Under his guidance and protection, his sheep are free from concern. Lacking nothing, they are free to be sheep: grazing, resting, and frolicking at will (see Psalm 23:1-3). They have only one responsibility. By necessity, they must remain attentive to their good shepherd's voice, heeding his every word. Ignoring all other voices, sheep follow only the one voice that they know: the voice of their shepherd (see John 10:1-6).

Sheep's ability to recognize and heed their shepherd's voice is crucial to the sheep's survival. Relatively weak and passive animals, sheep do not fend well for themselves. Left alone, they meander and are easily lost. Straying, they are helpless in the wild, getting stuck in bogs and eating things that are harmful. Not fast enough to outrun predators, strong enough to overpower them or smart enough to outwit them, sheep are sitting ducks---easy prey. Nor do large numbers *give* sheep the strength that they need for survival, for no matter how many sheep a flock contains, predators simply pick them off one at a time until they are gone.

To survive, sheep need a shepherd---a good one, for the shepherd is the sheep's only source of strength. The greater the shepherd's strength, the more invincible are the sheep in his care.

In the span of time between the days of Moses and the days of Jesus, Prophets of God would *receive* words from God that they would deliver to the Israelites to reveal the coming Savior as God's chosen Shepherd of God's "flock" (Family). In searching for the lost, bringing back strays, binding up the injured and providing for their feeding, Jesus would justly be their needed strength forever (see Ezekiel 34:11-16).

> He will stand and shepherd his flock in the strength of the LORD, in the majesty of the name of the LORD his God. And they will live securely, for then his greatness will reach to the ends of the earth. And he will be their peace. (Micah 5:4-5a)

Far more than strengthening, *God is Strength*... beginning to end, period.

# The Experiencing (The Israelite)

When the Israelites began their exodus from Egypt, they were a distinct multitude of people. Though probably not perfectly homogeneous, they were close. Related to most one another by blood, life experience and faith in God Jehovah, they most certainly had more in common with one another than not. The typical Israelite knew much about bondage, but little about freedom; much about promise, but little about fulfillment; much about hard work, but little about accomplishment.

For all the Israelite's life, he would have heard his family talk about a land outside of Egypt that was theirs by promise. The land had been *given* by God to Abraham, then to Isaac and then to Jacob. But the Israelite had never seen the land, for his entire life had been lived in a land that wasn't his. Different from the Egyptians in whose land he resided, he was scrutinized and degraded for both his lifestyle and his worship of God. In Egypt, he was a foreigner, an alien. Egypt was not his home. But life in Egypt was all that his family had known for generations. So, though the promise *gave* hope, his question was this: did he have any real chance of change occurring in his lifetime?

The Israelite couldn't have helped but think about the facts that had been passed down to him, especially the one of God's forewarning concerning Abraham's descendants. God had said that they would be oppressed in slavery in a strange land for four hundred years before finally *receiving* their land of promise (see Genesis 15:13-14). The Israelite knew firsthand that the oppression had indeed become reality, and by his family's count, four hundred years had passed. So if the story were true, where was the promise's fulfillment? Why were he and his family still living a life of bondage in Egypt? The Israelite must have surely pondered both the story's facts and God's faithfulness, wondering one thing: did he have any real hope of ever living free in the land that God had promised to *give* to them all?

Then came a day when a flicker of hope must have sparked anew in the Israelite, for news arrived that Moses had returned to Egypt with words from God. While Moses' previous palace life would have made his return big news to Israelite and Egyptian alike, even bigger news to the Israelite would have been Moses' assertion that he had returned by God's directive.

After speaking first to his brother, Aaron, and then to the Israelite elders (see Exodus 4:29-31), Moses had then gone to Pharaoh. Assisted by Aaron, Moses had delivered God's dictum to Pharaoh to "let the Israelites go out of his country" (Exodus 6:11). Then, to substantiate that the source of their words was God, not them, they had out-performed Pharaoh's top sorcerers and magicians in a head-to-head contest of wonders, *giving* Pharaoh a glimpse of the power of God that backed the words of the directive that they were delivering (see Exodus 7:8-13).

The Israelite must have pondered the totality of the news as being almost too good to be true. Dared he, of all people, hope that his generation would be the one to be set free? Was God not only real, but also concerned about him and his family? After so many years of oppression, he couldn't have helped but be skeptical about God actually rescuing them. So even though the ruling elders believed Moses, the Israelite found it difficult to ascertain the trustworthiness of a man whom he did not know personally (see Exodus 6:9). Still, there was something to be said for Moses being back among them, attempting to help them out.

A time would come when men's doubts regarding the trustworthiness of both Jesus and His words would generate even greater skepticism than that encountered by Moses in Egypt. Skeptic disbelief would cause men to forfeit freedom in their bondage to wrong thinking. Men would want proof that Jesus was from God, that He was speaking and acting in accordance with God's will by God-*given* authority to do so. Then one day, Jesus would directly address the issue, saying that miracles, signs and wonders from God would have to be seen in order for His words to be fully believed by men who doubted that He was indeed from God (see John 4:48).

Miracles, signs and wonders from God were the proof that not only the Israelites, but men of all ages, would need to overcome much disbelief. So, faithfully matching provision to need, God has regularly *given* all three in ways that are in man's best interest to *receive*. In the Israelite's time, plagues descended on Egypt right on cue. Frogs, flies and locusts arrived in hoards; a plague came on livestock, and boils came on men. Hail fell on crops, and darkness fell over a land of Egyptian idol-worshippers.

The undeniable Presence of God acting for the Israelites' welfare must have left the Israelite shell-shocked. By the time Moses issued a warning regarding a coming tenth plague, the Israelite's respectful fear of God Jehovah had increased so much that he sacrificed an unblemished lamb, smeared the lamb's blood on the doorposts of his home and had his family join him in eating all of the roasted meat, exactly as Moses had instructed.

But even as he stood in the midst of the bloody sacrifice that day, the Israelite must have considered how foolish, only weeks earlier, he would have considered his current actions to be. And yet, even as he was preparing the lamb, he must have wondered how a dead lamb could save lives. But then again, he would have remembered witnessing the nine previous plagues that had recently befallen Egypt. So to not do as Moses had said to do would be truly foolish. By faith then, the Israelite followed the instructions that he had *received*, for he had little choice but to trust the promise that had been *given*. He had to believe that his family would be saved by the blood of the lamb, whose life was ending by his hand, for he had no other viable option. As Moses trusted God, the Israelite had to trust Moses. The Israelite knew one thing for certain: if the death angel came, he couldn't save anyone. If God didn't save them, death would surely occur.

That evening, while securing his family behind the blood stained doorposts of their house, the question of the blood's effectiveness and the Israelite's obedience in trusting it must have loomed over all. But later that night, as the sound of anguished Egyptian cries confirmed the death angel's presence (see Exodus 12:29-30), God's words of promised protection were also confirmed by the fact that the Israelite and his family were all still alive. Immensely grateful, the Israelite could only have continuously thanked God for a dead lamb's blood that had somehow spared life.

By the time word reached the Israelite that Pharaoh was letting the Israelites go, the Israelite was willing to follow God by following Moses. Joining the orderly ranks that were forming, he was laden with gold, silver and clothing that were *given* to him by the Egyptians who were imploring the Israelites to leave their land immediately (see Exodus 12:33-36). Then, as the procession began to move forward, the Israelite headed into the wilderness in an experience that could only have been surreal.

The Israelite had no need to look back as he departed Egypt, for he knew all too well the life behind him. Little, though, did he know of the life ahead of him. Each step *took* him deeper into new territory, *giving* the Israelite new experience in greater awareness of God. But despite all that had transpired, the Israelite couldn't quite seem to shake a feeling of uncertainty about the God whose bigness and goodness he had wondered about all of his life. Having witnessed the plagues, he wanted to know if God would remain to continue doing only good for him.

Any time that the Israelite doubted God's Presence, he only had to look at the pillars of cloud and fire that led the way to be assured that God had not left them (see Exodus 13:21-22). The pillars were faith builders, reminders of the Israelite's newly discovered reality of God, a visual assurance of an ever-present God.

But then there came a moment when knowing that God was present wasn't enough. That moment occurred when the experience that seemed to be a dream come true became a waking nightmare. With the Red Sea blocking the way forward and the terrain hemming in the sides, the procession came to a dead stop. Turning around, the Israelite saw dust clouds from Pharaoh's approaching army closing in from behind (see Exodus 14:5-10).

Realizing that he had nowhere to go, fear gripped him, for he had little or no expectation of God intervening on his behalf. Forgetting altogether that God, not Moses, was leading, he joined others in shouting remorse at having followed Moses out of Egypt. "Moses answered the people, 'Do not be afraid. Stand firm and you will see the deliverance the LORD will bring you today. The Egyptians you see today you will never see again. The LORD will fight for you; you need only to be still'" (Exodus 14:13-14).

As the Israelite watched Moses extend his arm over the sea, the seemingly impossible occurred right before his eyes. Miraculously, the Israelite's fearful anger was transformed into astonished relief as he watched a sudden strong wind part the sea to materialize an escape route forward. The Israelite's way out of the impending death that threatened him was not to be on the sea, around the sea, above the sea, nor in the sea, but through the sea... unbelievably *through* the sea (see Exodus 14:21-31).

Stunned, the Israelite fell in step once again with the procession as it began moving forward. Passing between the walls of water that defined the way, the Israelite walked in unchartered territory, as he followed Moses across a dry seabed. But he wasn't alone. The walls held fast until every Israelite from first to last had safely crossed, and then more of the unexpected occurred. The now jubilant Israelite watched as the walls collapsed on Pharaoh and his entire army to destroy them all. The Israelite's escape route had been no less than the Egyptian's death trap.

At that particular moment in time, the Israelite's life was so far removed from his previous understanding of reality that he had no way of processing the events through prior experience to make sense of it all. So, in rationalizing the miraculous events as a one-time anomaly, not a new way of life with God, the Israelite was left with little expectation that God would continue to supernaturally provide for his every need, as God had always done, one way or another, beyond his knowledge.

But God did exactly that, making Himself---His goodness and His greatness---better known to the Israelite, again and again. To the Israelite's repeated astonishment, the farther that he walked with God, the more miracles that he witnessed and *received*. Miracles from God just kept occurring, when and as needed, despite the persistent grumbling that he and his family regularly did against Moses and, hence, against God (see Exodus 15:22-17:16).

Though the Israelite was sincerely remorseful at times regarding his lack of complete trust in God, he was never quite able to muster up the faith that he needed to get beyond the mindset of fear that had *taken* root in him in Egypt. Surrounded by Egyptian plenty in the midst of his need, he had learned to expect little good.

Still, each time that the Israelite failed to trust God to meet his needs, he fully determined and expected that he would do better the next time. As of then, the Israelite had little understanding that faith is a gift from God that is built up in ongoing relationship with Him. Faith is neither manufactured nor conjured up from within whenever it is needed, but increases in ongoing, affirmative interaction that strengthens it for times of need. Though the Israelite's faith in God had already grown to some degree, it still lacked the certainty that overcomes all doubt.

After the Israelite had witnessed the plagues in Egypt, he had trusted God enough to follow Him into a wilderness that was incapable of sustaining him. But only in that wilderness did he become more fully aware of his total dependence upon God for every aspect of life. The realization was a concern to the Israelite.

A day would come in the yet distant future when Jesus' life, death and resurrection would verify God's total commitment to all men, for God would *give* His all in Jesus. Jesus, knowing His Father's loving-goodness, would trust His Father fully, leading men to do likewise in their interactions with Him; for Jesus would speak not as Prophet, but as God's Son, whose expectation of God differed much from that of servants.

> Which of you, if his son asks for bread, will give him a stone? Or if he asks for a fish, will give him a snake? If you, then, though you are evil, know how to give good gifts to your children, how much more will your Father in heaven give good gifts to those who ask him! (Matthew 7:9-11)

Jesus would *give* men experience with the Truth of God that would counteract the doubt that fear conceives. The fear of God's abandonment of men in both life and death would be overcome by God's manifested loving-goodness in Jesus, for "perfect love drives out fear" (1 John 4:18b). Jesus would be both the "cornerstone" (Matthew 21:42; Mark 12:10; Luke 20:17) and the "sure foundation" (1 Corinthians 3:11) of men's faith in God. Jesus' rock solid, unshakable, immovable, steadfast, dependable, trustworthy, perfect faith in His Father would be men's enablement to trust God fully.

> The LORD is my rock, my fortress and my deliverer; My God is my rock, in whom I take refuge. He is my shield and the horn of my salvation, my stronghold. (Psalms 18:2)

A stronghold is a place of defense, a place of fortification that remains standing during attacks by the opposition. Its time-proven strength promises impenetrability. Though strongholds can be physical formations, offering protection from physical danger, others are mental strongholds that guard men's beliefs by keeping opposing beliefs at bay. The longer a belief has been in place, the more ingrained it has become through self-fortification, increasing its influence in decision-making. But while Truth-based beliefs grow stronger with every debate, those that are false are eventually demolished by Truth. Though some wrong beliefs can put up quite a fight on their way to extinction, their pretentious arguments cannot outlast eternal Truth.

Only Jesus, demolishing every wrong belief by upholding every right one, would be man's eternal stronghold---secure refuge, for Jesus is anchored in His Father. In the Garden of Gethsemane, Jesus would speak of trusting His earthly life to His Father, saying, "Father, if you are willing, take this cup from me; yet not my will, but yours be done" (Luke 22:42). On the Cross, He would trust His Father in death, as well, saying "Father, into your hands I commit my spirit" (Luke 23:46a).

Resurrection would be proof that Jesus' trust in His Father was completely valid (see John 2:19-21). An empty Tomb and a risen Christ would be evidence of a fully trustworthy God (see Matthew 28; Mark 16; Luke 24; John 20). Right trust of God would then be multiplied by the testimony of hundreds of eye witnesses, who would see the proof for themselves (see 1 Corinthians 15:3-8) and then pass on the Good News to others. One walking Miracle would do that which would have otherwise remained impossible for men. They would concede pride in right repentance to trust God through the finished work of the Cross of Jesus.

Far more than trustworthy, *God is Trust*... beginning to end, period.

# *The Trying* (The Law)

Man has been trying since Garden of Eden days to believe God, to have faith in God, to trust God unconditionally. But believing doesn't involve trying, for something or someone is either believed or not. "Trying to believe" means that though belief is desired, it has not yet been achieved. It does not exist.

Neither can faith be worked up, for faith is an action that is based on belief. It is a choice that demonstrates belief through a free will decision that is based on knowledge. Neither belief nor faith can be mandated, but rather are conclusions drawn from accumulated sensory information. A conclusion that is *accepted* as true is believed, and one that is *rejected* as either false or indeterminable is disbelieved. Apart from coercion, actions occur in accordance with belief and disbelief, regardless of whether the determinants used are accurate or not.

When the Israelites failed to trust God in the wilderness for all provision, their inability to do so was based on lifetimes of conflicting data regarding God. From their perspective, God had seemed to be either absent from or indifferent to their plight, creating a mixture of Truth and fallacy in their belief systems.

Oppression had been the Israelites' longtime reality, filling their senses and overloading their memories with painful emotional and physical experiences that were a certainty of life in Egypt. God's loving-goodness wasn't necessarily as obvious during the times of oppression. So no matter how diligently the Israelites tried to fully trust God later in the wilderness, painful memories kept skewing their conclusions toward doubt.

Doubt is a worrywart that steals peace of mind by demanding ongoing reassurance that faith finds unnecessary. The Israelites' doubt of God that had formed in Egypt created a desire for assurance that God would never again even appear to leave them. They wanted a guarantee from God that He would remain faithful to them, and they were willing to pay to get it.

The permanent peace with God that the Israelites wanted would eventually be purchased for mankind by Jesus---the only One capable of paying the bill. God would "... reconcile to himself all things, whether things on earth or things in heaven, by making peace through his blood, shed on the cross" (Colossians 1:20). The price of everlasting peace would be the blood of Jesus. But even after Jesus would purchase peace with God for men, it would still have to be *accepted* by faith. Faith cannot be bypassed by men in their relationships with God. The connection is clear.

> Therefore, since we have been justified by faith, we have peace with God through our Lord Jesus Christ, through whom we have gained access by faith into this grace in which we now stand. (Romans 5:1-2)

But the Israelites, not yet understanding the connection between faith and peace, fretted their way from one wilderness camp to the next, worrying about each upcoming need. Lacking comprehension about themselves and God, they determined to eliminate their doubt and fear by entering into a working agreement with God that would set parameters for both parties.

Used to working hard for others, the Israelites readily accepted the concept of working for personal gain, revealing a greater faith in rules than relationship. Misguided, they assumed that a business-like arrangement with God would be mineable to them both.

Expecting to satisfy God with their good behavior by strictly adhering to performance-based standards meant to the Israelites that God would be required to then be faithful to them, *giving* them peace of mind. With little forethought as to the wisdom, feasibility, practicality or consequence of such an arrangement, they relished a chance to regulate their relationship with God.

God knew, of course, that the certainty that the Israelites wanted is found only in an unchanging God, who was already with them and for them. The Israelites had exactly what they needed; they just didn't believe so. So once more, God acted in man's best interest. By *giving* the Israelites what they wanted, He *gave* them what they needed: opportunity to learn the Truth firsthand. The experience would be most enlightening.

From the moment when Adam and Eve exited the Garden of Eden until the Israelites arrived at the foot of Mt. Sinai on their wilderness journey, man had no formally stated laws or regulations from God to uphold. None... Not one. Every blessing of provision had come to man by means of God's grace alone. Man had never earned any bit of God's life-sustaining and/or life-enhancing provisions, and he never could or would.

But less than two months after the Israelites left Egypt, while camped in front of Mt. Sinai (see Exodus 12:1-3, 19:1), *receiving* God's unconditional provision, they murmured nonstop against God. Dissatisfied with having to depend upon God's grace, they wanted the proverbial "more." They looked right past God's abundance to fear lack, not comprehending that, with God, lack does not exist. Even when God would want to *give* them the Promised Land, "flowing with milk and honey" (Numbers 14:8), they would bemoan the gift as a death trap and refuse to *take* it. Focused on need, they couldn't see supply.

So God *gave* the Israelites the "more" that they wanted: an abundance of words to which they could try to comply at God's level of perfection. Referring to them here in totality as the Law, the full repertoire of instructions (commands, laws and decrees) that the Israelites *received* (see Deuteronomy 5:31; Leviticus 1-27) would *give* them guidance and organization while keeping them simultaneously busy trying to uphold and clarify the Law's countless nuances for many generations to come.

Ironically, the same people who doubted the faithfulness of God were so thoroughly convinced of their own ability to be completely faithful to Him that they *accepted* the Law sight unseen.

The Israelites had neither *received* the stone tablets containing the Law's Ten Commandments (see Exodus 20:1-17; Deuteronomy 5:1-22) nor been told of any of the Law's entirety when they unilaterally *accepted* it all with great pride. "The people all responded together, 'We will do everything the LORD has said'" (Exodus 19:8a). Jumping at an opportunity to be made "a kingdom of priests and a holy nation" (Exodus 19:6), the Israelites entered into blood covenant with God, confident that they could do all that God required of them (see Exodus 24:1-8).

But their inability to remain faithful to God surfaced immediately. Even as Moses was on the mountain, watching God etch the Ten Commandments in stone with His Finger, the Israelites were idolizing the work of their hands by worshipping a golden calf that they molded in Moses' absence. When Moses returned to witness the Israelites' blatant and sinful worship of themselves above God, he cast down the stone tablets that he was carrying, shattering them and their written commands. The act was a powerful visual aid for the stern reprimand and consequences that, by Law, had to follow (see Exodus 32).

The Bible records not a single Israelite death as having occurred during the trip from Egypt to Mt. Sinai. Yet on the day when the Commandments were handed down from God by way of Moses, three thousand Israelites died by the sword at the hand of the Levites---the tribe of Moses that descended from Jacob's son Levi. The Levites were the only Israelites who chose to stand with Moses for the LORD that day in opposition to the sinful behavior of even their brothers and sons (see Exodus 32:25-29). Their action set them apart from the other tribes to make them Israel's future assistants to the priests, who would all be Aaron's descendants (see Numbers 3:10-11, 8:11-19). Other individuals who had also sinned against God that day, but were not slain, were later to *receive* a promised plague (see Exodus 32:33-35).

The question arises as to how a good and loving God could strike down so many people for whom He so greatly cared and then reward those who did the slaying. But, in actuality, God didn't strike anyone. The Israelites did, not by God's desire, but by the judgment of the Law to which the Israelites had all fully agreed. The Law was a contract, a binding agreement, and it contained penalty clauses set by God for breaking the contract. Whereas mercy could have made exception by grace, the justice that the Law demanded could not. The Israelites had to abide by the agreement, enforcing it, or be equally guilty of breaking it.

The Law depicted God's holy perfection (see Romans 7:12). Right and holy itself, the Law was perfect, but the Israelites were not. Try as they might to imitate God's holiness by following the Law's requirements, the Israelites' lack of godliness showed continually. Consequently, their short-sightedness regarding their limitations (the very thing that they were trying to overcome) separated them from God by the sins that they committed in failing to perfectly uphold the Law that they had wanted. The Law had the reverse effect from that which they had expected. In trying to buy peace of mind, the Israelites had only burdened themselves with the endless striving of trying not to break the Law that controlled them.

Breakage of the Law was not measured in degrees, but in absolutes, for rules are either kept or they are not. All sin is equally wrong. "Everyone who sins breaks the law; in fact, sin is lawlessness" (1 John 3:4). Other translations say "... sin is the transgressions of the law" (KJV), "... sin is the breaking of law" (HCSB), "... sin is disobedience" (ISV). In summation: "All wrongdoing is sin" (1 John 5:17a).

While perfect adherence to holy living by the Law guaranteed blessings that *give* life, sinful living's deviation from the Law guaranteed curses that lead to death (see Deuteronomy 28). In the Garden of Eden, where Adam and Eve had deviated from the one and only God-*given* rule by which Adam was to live, sin had entered man, cursing him with death. Sin's consequence, of which God had rightly forewarned Adam, was not God's desire for anyone. So, as God had wanted to bless Adam, God also wanted to bless the Israelites, and He said so.

> This day I call heaven and earth as witnesses against you that I have set before you life and death, blessings and curses. Now choose life so that you and your children may live. (Deuteronomy 30:19)

Right living according to the Law in order to earn blessings required the Israelites' fulltime attention to the Law's demands, which were even more extensive than they first appeared. Beyond sins of commission, sins of omission were also important (see James 4:17), for as God is holy and does only good all of the time, so should man do likewise.

> The LORD said to Moses, "Speak to the entire assembly of Israel and say to them, 'Be holy because I, the LORD your God, am holy.'" (Leviticus 19:1-2)

The Law's expectation of perfection made no allowance for even a man's ignorance of the Law. The Bible's first recorded stoning to death of a man after the Law was *received* apparently involved such an infraction. The man condemned to death was guilty of no more than picking up firewood on the Sabbath (see Numbers 15:32-36). Most probably, he had done so at will at other times in his life prior to the Law without consequence, for there had been no consequence. But under the Law, the act was considered to be work, which desecrated the Sabbath day that the Law designated for rest. By Law, as God had rested on the seventh day following Creation (see Genesis 2:2), so was man to rest every seventh day to honor God. Hence, picking up firewood on the Sabbath was sinful. It shouldn't have been done.

During the coming ministry of Jesus, this particular infringement of the Law would regularly be used by the Pharisees and the teachers of the Law to condemn Jesus' work of healing people on the Sabbath. On one Sabbath day while in a synagogue, Jesus would free a woman from a crippling spirit of infirmity, only to have His act of compassion reprimanded.

Indignant because Jesus had healed on the Sabbath, the synagogue ruler said to the people, "There are six days for work. So come and be healed on those days, not on the Sabbath." The Lord answered him, "You hypocrites! Doesn't each of you on the Sabbath untie his ox or donkey from the stall and lead it out to give it water? Then should not this woman, a daughter of Abraham, whom Satan has kept bound for eighteen long years, be set free on the Sabbath day from what bound her?" (Luke 13:14-16)

The Law was hard and fast in its regulation of men's relationships with both God and one another. It even structured men's worship of God. By Law, the Israelites were obligated to sacrificial acts of thanksgiving and worship, plus designated feast days and rituals. The prescribed worship, though a poor substitute for the heart-generated kind, was *given* to men as an intermediary step to God attaining the intimacy with men that He desires.

While man tends to quantitatively measure the productivity of his acts, deeds and works that can include worship, God is more concerned with the quality of the underlying motivation for the productiveness. Contrary to worldly belief, right action does not make a man right with God. Rather, the reverse is true. Right alignment of a man's heart to that of God produces right action that flows from the right decision that a man makes to allow God to make him into a greater likeness of God. Being so changed increases a man's godly concern for all of the world, superseding by far the self-promotion that often lies behind actions done by a man in order to feel good or look good to self and others.

The LORD does not look at the things man looks at. Man looks at the outward appearance, but the LORD looks at the heart. (1 Samuel 16:7b)

Why then, if God, in knowing the hearts and minds of men, knew that the Israelites were incapable of keeping the Law, did the Law command death, especially death by stoning? How could the pelting of men to death with stones be associated in any way with a good, loving God or be in man's best interest?

Consider this: stones represent legalistic hearts that are hard, cold, unforgiving. As the Law allowed for no mitigating circumstances, nor showed mercy, neither did people who chose to live by the Law. Under the Law, individuals held each other accountable to standards that they themselves could not maintain. The Law held men to an inflexible perfection that was as rigid as the stones on which the Ten Commandments were etched (see Exodus 32:16, 34:1). Unbendable, the Law was easily broken.

While stoning itself is reprehensible, the fact that the Israelites willingly did so made its use good, for stoning disclosed the condition of men's hearts and minds. A man's willingness to stone others was tangible evidence of a cold heart that misjudged itself to be more righteous than others. The stoning to death of those who were known to be guilty under the Law was only accomplished by those whose sins remained yet hidden.

When the Israelite assembly stoned to death the man who had picked up sticks on the Sabbath day, every participant revealed a self-righteous, holier-than-thou attitude that belied judgment of others as an entitlement of personal responsibility in denouncing sin. Stoning forced prideful men to consider the question that confronted them all in stoning: "You who brag about the law, do you dishonor God by breaking the law?" (Romans 2:23).

Because the Israelites had collectively decided to attempt to live sin-free according to the Law, they were also collectively responsible for upholding it. Any sin that entered their camp endangered them all, for sin is easily multiplied by temptation. Therefore, strict enforcement of the Law was a matter of self-preservation. Each stone thrown revealed a heart that was more concerned for self than others. Stoning was personal... *very* personal.

During the years immediately following Jesus' earthly ministry, a man named Saul of Tarsus would one day hold the belongings of men who, according to the Law, would be justly stoning to death a man named Stephen (see Acts 7). Stephen would be guilty of being a sold-out follower of Jesus Christ; while Saul—a religious, sold-out zealot of the Law (see Philippians 3:4-6)—would consider it his responsibility to persecute Christians who were not abiding by the Law. But a personal encounter with the resurrected Jesus would change Saul's thinking in a flash (see Acts 9:1-30), *giving* Saul (known from then on as Paul) a new heart that would be willing to be stoned for the sake of others with whom he would share the Gospel (see Acts 14:19)—the very act of heresy for which Saul had assented to Stephen's stoning.

The loving-goodness of God that would be revealed in Jesus would be life transforming, producing by grace the right living that the Law could not produce by demand. Empowerment to live God's way would come via the Holy Spirit, the third Person of the Godhead. Arriving after Jesus' ascension, Holy Spirit would remain to dwell in Christians, *giving* them opportunity to *receive* abundant life through Truth's revelation.

In contrast to the three thousand people who died upon the Law's arrival at Mt. Sinai, Holy Spirit's arrival would lead to three thousand people *receiving* eternal life in Christ Jesus on that one day alone (see Acts 2:1-41). From that day forward, Holy Spirit would deliver Truth to the world through the changed hearts and minds of men who would be transformed by the *receiving* of God's grace through faith. By first *giving* the Law to reveal the extent of men's need for grace, God prepared men's hearts to *receive* His grace that Jesus would extend to all.

> For the law was given through Moses; grace and truth came through Jesus Christ. (John 1:17)

A day would arrive when the Truth of God's grace revealed in Jesus' compassion would demonstrate, as it regularly would, divine superiority over legalism. Speaking to a crowd that would be ready to stone a woman caught in adultery, Jesus would challenge all men, saying, "If any one of you is without sin, let him be the first to throw a stone at her" (John 8:7b). His words would be a reminder of all men's personal need for mercy.

Do not judge, or you too will be judged. For in the same way you judge others, you will be judged, and with the measure you use, it will be measured to you. (Matthew 7:1-2)

The crowd surrounding the woman would disperse, one by one, leaving the woman to face Jesus alone. "'Then neither do I condemn you,' Jesus declared. 'Go now and leave your life of sin'" (John 8:11). The only person who could rightly judge the woman, wouldn't. Instead, He would *give* her the mercy that she needed to live, when she needed it: while she was guilty in sin.

An eye-for-an-eye and a tooth-for-a-tooth system of justice is the world's *modus operandi*, not God's. God wants "… mercy, not sacrifice, and acknowledgement of God rather than burnt offerings" (Hosea 6:6). Jesus would quote this verse (see Matthew 9:13a, 12:7), adding, "I have not come to call the righteous, but sinners" (Matthew 9:13b; see also Mark 2:17; Luke 5:32).

Any man who wrongly believes himself to be righteously good enough by any moral code will never see a need to humble himself to be saved. A man's ignorance of his need for salvation can condemn him to a death that he never sees coming (see Hosea 4:6).

Similarly, men who live by a mixture of law and grace cheat themselves and others out of abundant provision of God's grace in this world and/or the next. As mixing oil and water prevents either from being used beneficially, so does mixing grace and legalism negate their benefits (see Galatians 3:3). If grace is *accepted*, law is not needed. Likewise, if law is fulfilled, there is no need for grace.

Trying to live simultaneously by both nullifies the good that either does, leaving men without profit.

The Law that can appear harsh was not *given* by a demanding God to good and loving men, but instead was *received* by demanding men from a good and loving God. A day would come, though, when the Law would meet its match. Jesus would righteously fulfill the Law for all men (see Matthew 5:17). By removing sin from the equation that sentences men to death, Jesus would use the power of the Law to *give* victory to life (see 1 Corinthians 15:54-57). By men's confessions of faith in Jesus, they would be raised out of their deaths to live in His life.

> For it is with your heart that you believe and are justified, and it is with your mouth that you confess and are saved. (Romans 10:10)

But before men could willingly *receive* Jesus as Savior, God would first use the Law to lead them to *accept* the necessity of substitutionary atonement. While the suffering of all men for the sin of the one man Adam would be considered unfair by some, the idea of God's sinless Son dying to pay for all men's sin would be much more difficult for men to *accept* as being right by God.

So by God's good grace, the Law's totality was far more than a basic set of rules that defined men's good behavior. It *gave* everything that was needed then and there: the temporary covering of men's sins by the blood of animals that were to be sacrificed in men's places; an altar for immediately beginning sacrificial worship of God (see Exodus 20:24-26); and permanent housing for the Law's stone tablets in the Ark of the Covenant, which was to reside in the Holy of Holies---the inner most sanctuary of the Tabernacle, all built to specific proportions (see Exodus 25-26). It also provided detailed instructions for making the clothing that was to be worn by the priests whenever they represented the Israelites before God (see Exodus 28).

The Law even included a means for Israel's High Priest to approach God in the Holy of Holies and seek God's mercy for the entire Israelite nation on a yearly basis (see Leviticus 16). By Law, the properly attired High Priest had to begin his petition by making proper sacrifice at the Tabernacle's outer court altar. Then, by fulfilling other requirements, he would move deeper into the Tabernacle until he would stand before God's Mercy Seat atop the Ark, which held the commandments inside. There, a righteous God, who literally sat above the Law, was able to *give* mercy to all who the priest in right standing represented.

For a man to enter the Holy of Holies improperly, at will, was a death sentence. So was touching the Ark that held God's seat. In a time yet to come during the days of King David, an Israelite named Uzzah would reach out to steady the Ark during transport to keep it from falling (see 2 Samuel 6:6-7). Though Uzzah's intention may have been good, according to men's evaluation of his action, his disrespect of God's holy perfection presumed prideful equality with God that caused Uzzah to drop dead on the spot. Infringement was that serious. Unrighteousness cannot stand in God's holy Presence.

A day would come in history, between the time of King David and the time of Jesus, when Esther, a Jew by birth and a queen by marriage, would defy protocol of the law of the land where she was living in Persia. With good intent, she would approach the king uninvited. The ordained penalty for dishonoring both the king and the law in that manner would be death. Mercy alone would spare first Esther's life and then the lives of all of the Jews in Persia for whom she would plea. The mercy that she would *receive*, overriding the death penalty, would be *given* to her for only one reason: her intimate relationship with her husband, who also happened to be king. Though her husband would want to forgive her, only the king would have the legal right by law to do so (see Esther 4:1-5:2).

In a time that is yet to come, all men will stand before God in need of mercy. Those who will try to do so in their own righteousness will experience unimaginable trepidation as they *receive* due justice by law. But those who approach God as Christ's righteous Bride (see Revelation 19:7) ---God's Universal Church Family, united with Jesus in Holy Communion---will stand in the hope *given* to them in their intimate relationship with Jesus. As King (see Revelation 19:16), Jesus will have the authority---the legal right by Law---to save His Bride from death. The mercy factor that will allow Him to do so will be His Blood, shed upon the altar of the Cross to redeem His Bride by Law.

The Law allowed for blood-bought redemption because "the life of a creature is in the blood" (Leviticus 17:11a). By Law, the blood of sacrificed animals had to be sprinkled on men and objects to cleanse them from impurity, for the Law required "that nearly everything be cleansed with blood, and without the shedding of blood there is no forgiveness" (Hebrews 9:22).

But impure animal blood was insufficient in providing permanent relief from sin "because it is impossible for the blood of bulls and goats to take away sins" (Hebrews 10:4). Unable to remove sin, animal blood simply covered the sin that was present in a surface-like cleansing. But the sin within men remained ever-present, and the covering quickly faded with additional sin.

The Blood of Jesus, though, would be different from all other. Sin-free, it alone would be perfectly pure (see Hebrews 4:15; 1 Peter 2:22). Sinless, Jesus would *take* the world's sin (past, present and future) upon His body (see Isaiah 53:12; John 1:29), carrying it with Him into death to fulfill the Law's requirements for justice (see Colossians 2:13-14). But being perfectly righteous Himself, Jesus would pass through death, for death would have no legal right to hold Him (see Acts 2:24). Then, leaving sin buried in death, He would walk out of the Tomb in eternal life. As everlasting High Priest, Jesus would intercede forever for all who would rightly trust Him to represent them before God.

> When Christ came as high priest of the good things that are already here, he went through the greater and more perfect tabernacle that is not man-made, that is to say, not a part of this creation. He did not enter by means of the blood of goats and calves, but he entered the Most Holy Place once for all by his own blood, having obtained eternal

redemption. The blood of goats and bulls and the ashes of a heifer sprinkled on those who are ceremonially unclean sanctify them so that they are outwardly clean. How much more, then, will the blood of Christ, who through the eternal Spirit offered himself unblemished to God, cleanse our consciences from acts that lead to death, so that we may serve the living God! (Hebrews 9:11-14)

God has been using blood sacrifice to cleanse men's consciences from guilt since man first sinned in the Garden of Eden. There, sudden awareness within Adam and Eve of the sinful nature that they had *received* by free will choice created shame. Unable to undo the sin that they had committed, they attempted to hide their guilt from God and one another by covering their exposed selves with available leaves (see Genesis 3:7). But then God *gave* them something better.

> The LORD God made garments of skins for Adam and his wife and clothed them. (Genesis 3:21)

God covered Adam and Eve with skins that cost animal life, pointing ahead to the grace of God's good and perfect plan of salvation in Jesus---the last Adam (see 1 Corinthians 15:45). The Garden covering held for centuries, until men chose to *take* on the responsibility for their covering by trying to fulfill the Law. But no matter how deep the blood of sacrificed animals ran, its effectiveness was minuscule compared to that which would run from the Cross. The righteousness of Jesus would *give* men permanent respite from trying in vain to do that which only God can do: *righteously fulfill the Law* (see Matthew 5:17) *and righteously forgive all who cannot* (see Acts 13:38).

One day Jesus would tell a parable about a servant, who owed a king an exorbitant debt that was impossible for him to pay by any means. By all rights, the servant should have gone to debtor's prison for life. But the king, *giving* unwarranted mercy, forgave the servant's entire debt and set the man free. But in doing so, the king expected the servant to treat his personal debtors likewise, forgiving all that was owed to the servant by others. Otherwise the servant would owe an outstanding debt of mercy to all. In depriving others of forgiveness, the servant would deprive himself of the same (see Matthew 18:21-35).

After concluding the parable, Jesus would warn that men who refuse to *give* mercy to one another, forgiving every wrong, cannot *receive* their Heavenly Father's forgiveness. Anyone who does not *receive* life by grace falls under law's jurisdiction by default. Jesus would emphasize so in the Lord's Prayer that He would model for His disciples (see Mathew 6:12; Luke 11:4).

But an important distinction must be noted between the king's hypothetical forgiveness in the parable and God's actual forgiveness through Jesus. Whereas the imaginary king simply waived the debt owed to him, foregoing justice, God cannot righteously do so. God's righteousness necessitates that the debt owed to Him by all men for sin against Him would have to be paid with His Son's perfectly righteous, priceless Blood.

As a result, all men would owe God a different kind of debt: one of freely *giving* to others in everlasting gratitude for the life of Jesus that would be freely *given* to them. In personally *accepting* Jesus as God's merciful Sacrifice, men would become God's extended provision of mercy in this world, enabling others to freely *give* in the same manner as they had *received*: sacrificially.

Far more than sacrificing, *God is Sacrifice*... beginning to end, period.

# The Taking (Joshua)

*A*ccepting a gift, especially one involving sacrifice, isn't always easy. Sometimes a gift's intended recipient harbors or feigns feelings of unworthiness that hinder the gift's *acceptance*. Sometimes hesitancy comes from questioning the giver's motives in *giving*. Sometimes lack of familiarity with the gift itself causes its offering simply to be unappreciated and discounted. But sometimes a gift just seems too good to be true and is, therefore, never *taken* due to disbelief.

During the Israelites' second year of wilderness living, Moses sent twelve men, one from each tribe, into the Promised Land of Canaan to spy out the land and assess the cities and the people (see Deuteronomy 1:19-25; Numbers 13). He did so by the Israelites' own prompting, not by God's direction. Though God had already told the Israelites that He was *giving* them a land that was good, the spies went out and gathered information for forty days to see for themselves and make their own analysis. Then, upon returning, each spy reported what he had seen.

In *giving* their personal assessments, the men uniformly agreed that the land was bountiful, the cities were fortified and the people were big and strong. The spies concurred that Canaan was indeed a land of prosperity, as God had said. But when it came to advising the nation on a plan of action, their opinions differed. Ten emphatically advised against trying to *take* Canaan, deeming the task far too dangerous... impossible, in fact. Focused on the size of their enemies, they looked at Canaan and saw only defeat. But the other two men---Joshua from the tribe of Ephraim and Caleb from the tribe of Judah---enthusiastically advised that, with God, the Israelites could surely *take* Canaan for their own, as God had said. Focused on the size of their God, they looked at Canaan and saw only victory.

Unfortunately, the Israelite nation did not have a faith in God to match that of Joshua and Caleb. After the people heard of the Canaanites' size and strength, they heard little else, for fear seized them and *took* control of their decision making. Unanimously, they refused to *take* the Promised Land that was theirs by God having said that He was *giving* it to them. United in their opposition to God's plan, the disgruntled Israelites complained bitterly about the leadership of Moses and Aaron, once again forgetting that God was the One doing the leading.

The Israelites did not get a new leader, as they wanted, but they did get a new promise from God: no man of fighting age (20 years or older), who had refused to *take* Canaan, would ever step foot in the Promised Land. The Israelites would remain in the wilderness another thirty-eight years as wanderers, never having a place to put down roots (see Deuteronomy 1:26-46).

The lengthy delay (see Deuteronomy 2:14) was a self-imposed one, for the Israelites' fear-driven decision not to go in left them with nowhere to go. So God used the time to raise a generation free from the doubt and fear that inhabited their parents. Growing up in continual awareness of God's Presence, they did not inherit their parents' negative mindset that kept their parents from *receiving* the blessing that God was *giving*. Instead, the young wanderers grew up wanting to go home.

The one thing that was needed in order for them to do so was faith in God. Everything else was secondary. Their parents had lacked the faith to go into Canaan with God and *take* the land from the various idol worshippers who were living there. Having spent most of their lives under the control of Egyptian idol worshippers from whom they had been unable to free themselves, they weren't able to imagine themselves conquering large Canaanite adversaries. Having miraculously escaped oppression once, they weren't willing to risk *giving* up the life that they had, not even to *take* God's offer of a better one.

The Israelites' meager thinking concerning God kept them from *receiving* the victory that God promised to *give*. Their declaration that they would be defeated in battle was true, for their words were self-fulfilling. The exodus generation defeated themselves by surrendering to the doubt and fear that oppressed them from within. The Canaanites were not the Israelites' greatest opposition; their wrong thinking was.

A day would come in the future when a boy named David, who would one day be king of Israel, would face a giant Philistine idol worshipper by the name of Goliath, who no other Israelite would be willing to fight (see 1 Samuel 17). Intimidated by Goliath's size and full regalia of bronze battle gear, the Israelites would envision only their own demise. But David's mindset would see only opportunity to *give* God greater glory in victory over such a puffed up blasphemer. While the Israelite army would define defeat in terms of their abilities, David would define victory in terms of God's. Doing so, David couldn't lose.

David would go into battle against Goliath fully outfitted, but not the world's way. Equipped by God with faith in the Name of the One with whom he would fight, David's only weapon would be a shepherd's slingshot that he regularly used to protect his father's flock. One rock slung by David in alignment with God's will would make Goliath's size inconsequential and his armor worthless, for the rock would penetrate the point of Goliath's greatest vulnerability: his forehead, behind which lay all of his wrong thinking.

Centuries after David's time, the Apostle Paul would describe the spiritual battle gear that is worn by men who *receive* salvation in Christ Jesus. Salvation itself would be everlasting covering, enabling men to do battle against evil without fear of death. Empowered with Truth, they would remain standing in peace with God to righteously counter all wrong thinking. Faith would shield them from temptation, and the Word of God would cut down lies and deception of every size. Spirit led battles would be Spirit won, *giving* God eternal glory in eternal victory (see Ephesians 6:14-18).

Every victory of any size of right over wrong *gives* God glory, but God is masterful at displaying His might in men's weakness (see 2 Corinthians 12:9). Many times throughout Israel's future history, God would purposefully send Israelites into battle outnumbered, outsized and/or underarmed to affirm that victory is from God, not men. Gideon would defeat the entire Midianite army with a small band of three hundred men armed only with empty pots, bugles and torches (see Judges 6). Jonathan---the son of Israel's future King Saul---and his armor-bearer would slay twenty Philistines within a half-acre of ground atop a rocky cliff that the two would first scale by hand in order to fight (see 1 Samuel 14:1-14). Mighty Men (Josheb-Basshebeth, slaying eight hundred; Eleazar; Shammah and others) would each single-handedly strike down massive numbers of Israel's opponents to attain victory with God (see 2 Samuel 23:8-12).

The more disproportionately small God's army of men would be in comparison to the enemy confronting them, the greater would be the end glory *given* to God for the victory attained God's way. Greater opponents, as so measured by any standard, would present not greater challenge, but greater opportunity for the Truth of God to outshine men's self-pride.

Teaching men to fight to bring down evil God's way, by *taking* a stand for good in full dependence upon God, would begin in earnest with the *taking* of Canaan. The task required a leader prepared by God for the specific purpose of leading a new generation of willing Israelites forward in obedience to God. Moses' right-hand man, Joshua (one of the two men who had wanted to *take* Canaan almost forty years earlier), fit the need perfectly. Caleb (the other spy who had had faith in God), still strong at eighty-five, was also to be honored to fight alongside Joshua to *take* their homeland together (see Joshua 14:6-15).

Moses, though, was not going to enter the Promised Land. His job assignment was complete. Instead, he was going Home to God. But before he did, God *gave* him opportunity to see the reality of the land that he had *accepted* by faith. God made a way for Moses to see the promise that God had made.

God made the decision, as always, with good and right reason. Years earlier, on the wilderness journey, Moses' sister had recently died, and the Israelites were disgruntled. In a weak moment, Moses had failed to comply with God. Instead of speaking to a rock in order to obtain water from it, as God had told Moses to do (see Numbers 20:1-13), Moses had chosen to strike the rock as he had done once before under a different directive from God (see Exodus 17:1-7). Not only was Moses' disobedience sinful, but it also had consequences, one being the undermining of Israelite confidence.

To be led successfully in battle in *taking* Canaan, the Israelites needed a leader whose directives they would believe without question were fully compliant with God's instructions. The man prepared by God to fill the need was none other than Joshua. Having wanted to have *taken* Canaan when God had first offered it, but then had waited patiently for thirty-eight years to do so through no fault of his own, Joshua was the man whom the Israelites would not doubt was following God in *taking* their homeland God's way. Joshua's longstanding trust in God in this matter enabled him to lead.

The decision to not allow Moses to enter the Promised Land (see Deuteronomy 34:1-8) was in the Israelites' best interest for at least two reasons. An able leader who wanted to *take* Canaan was needed, and Moses' disrespect of God had legal consequence that could not be overlooked. The best way forward was for Moses to go honorably Home to God, for his time to lead was up, he had successfully delivered, and for Joshua to boldly step up, for his time to lead had come.

*Taking* Canaan required a boldness generated by faith in God that presents itself in battle as courageous determination. So essential was Israelite boldness in displaying the faith needed for victory that three times God issued the same command to Joshua, saying, "Be strong and courageous" (Joshua 1:6, 9). Plus, an additional time, He added the word *very* before *courageous* for emphasis (Joshua 1:7). So fully did Joshua *receive* the words that he passed them on to the men who God was preparing to fight alongside of him under God's direction (see Joshua 1:18).

The boldness needed would only come from God-*given* faith in God. So God *gave* the Israelites specific encouragement before sending them into battle. The battle's outcome would not be determined by fighting ability, but by mindset. If the men stuck with God, doing things His way, they would win, for God couldn't lose. But if in doubting God, they chose to fight their own way, they would lose. Without God, they couldn't win.

The first specific encouragement was *given* by God to the Israelites during their crossing of the Jordan River to enter Canaan. There, God backed up flood waters to make a dry path for the Israelites to walk on, as He had done for their parents in the miraculous Red Sea crossing. The experience affirmed that the God who had delivered the Israelites out of oppression was still with them, delivering them safely home (see Joshua 3).

Then, during three specified days just prior to the Israelites *taking* Jericho (the first city *taken* in *taking* Canaan), God further encouraged Israelite faith in Him. The first day, God instructed all men of fighting age to be circumcised. Thereby each man *received* a personal sign of assurance that God was with him. Being identified with God in such a tangible way fulfilled covenant Law, removed past shame, increased a right sense of worth and dignified Israelite boldness in *taking* land that God said was theirs by inheritance of the promise (see Joshua 5:1-9).

Boldness dares to do that which timidity won't consider. It does what is necessary to rightly move ahead. It *accepts* risk, looking beyond adversity, in order to gain ground. It overcomes fear, conquering foes, holding nothing in reserve. Boldness allows no backing down and no turning around. It enables men to stand, until their enemies fold. Godly boldness requires a confidence in self that relies solely upon right confidence in God.

So the day after the circumcising was complete, God used the timely Passover celebration to continue emboldening the Israelites. In recalling the original Passover in Egypt that had saved their family from death, the Israelites were further strengthened in faith to believe that God would protect them from death in battle. The knowledge *gave* them courage that would keep them moving unhesitatingly forward with God (see Joshua 5:10).

Then on the day that followed Passover, God further encouraged the Israelites to continue moving ahead with Him by having them eat from the abundance of Canaan's good produce and grain. For the first time, they were fed with the God-*given* provisions of their homeland (see Joshua 5:11-12). The next day, the manna that had been their sustenance for many years stopped falling (see Exodus 16). Without it, the Israelites could not return to wilderness living. They had to move on or perish.

Strengthened in heart, mind and body by God, the Israelites were fully prepared to successfully battle God's opponents, God's way. They could envision the victory that was already theirs by promise. But even so, God still had one more assurance to *give* to the Israelites before commencing the battle.

As the Israelite army headed toward Jericho, God delivered a final message of encouragement to Joshua and the men fighting under him. He *gave* them assurance of Joshua's leadership under God's direction via words personally delivered to Joshua by the commander of the LORD's army. Filled with divine purpose, the words were reminiscent of Moses' first encounter with God at the burning bush, when God had said, "Take off your sandals, for the place where you are standing is holy ground" (Exodus 3:5b). By Joshua hearing those same words spoken to him, he *received* affirmation that God was with him as God had been with Moses. As God had prepared Moses in His Presence to follow God's unusual instructions over the ensuing years of deliverance, so did God prepare Joshua to *accept* His unusual battle plan for *taking* Jericho (see Joshua 5:13-6:5).

When the Israelite army arrived at Jericho, they found the well-fortified city tightly locked up, for the reputation of the God who was leading the Israelites had gone ahead to create more than a ripple of panic. Just prior to the Israelites having crossed the Jordan, Joshua had sent two spies to Jericho to gather information about the city (see Joshua 2). Later, those spies reported that Rahab, a prostitute whose home was in the city's wall, had hid the spies in order to protect them. From her, they had learned that the entire city feared the Israelites' God.

The fear of God that caused the inhabitants of Jericho to lock up their city played straight into God's battle plan. God didn't need Jericho's doors to be opened in order for the Israelites to enter the city and *take* it for their own. He just needed opportunity to prove that He can't be kept out of all that is rightly His. With Jericho being part of God's Creation, God's victory of it was eternally certain. The city was in His hands.

So God *took* Jericho as His rightful possession His way, without the Israelites lifting a hand to cause it to fall. The battle was

God's, and He justly claimed all of the plunder for His own glory. Jericho---the first fruit in *taking* Canaan---was dedicated to God, not to the men who were with Him (see Joshua 6:18-19).

The Israelites were able to share in God's victory only because of the bold faith that God had built up in them to do the seemingly absurd at His command. They hadn't needed worldly boldness to charge the city, as men would have been likely to have done. Instead they had needed the boldness to obey God when His instructions sounded nonsensical, irrelevant and ineffective in achieving the desired goal. The battle that they won, *giving* them Jericho, was the one of faith versus doubt, and they won it in obedience to God. In effect, they won a lot more than a city. They won a new life---the one God had promised.

During the battle, the Israelites had followed the precise instructions that Joshua had *received* from God. After they had marched in silence around the city for seven days straight, they had concluded their final go-round with a shout of acclamation of praise to God. The entire time, seven priests and the Ark of the Covenant had led the procession, and the army had followed. Each day, the droning of marching feet had elevated the fear level within the city that had become a prison to its inhabitants. Then, when the Israelites' praise had gone up to God, fulfilling obedience to God's instructions, the city walls had come down to fulfill God's promise to them: God *gave* Jericho to the Israelites so that they could *take* it for their own (see Joshua 6:12-21).

A day would come during the Church's early missionary days following Jesus' ascension when Paul and his missionary companion, Silas, would come under attack by men who would try to prevent their mission from continuing. The two would be imprisoned for acting in accordance with their faith in God by witnessing for Christ Jesus. But in that dark prison, at midnight, they would sing hymns---songs of praise---to God. As they would praise God, an earthquake would miraculously shake their shackles free from the prison's foundation (see Acts 16:16-34). Paul and Silas would be free to go, but they wouldn't leave. In staying, another miracle would occur:   the jailer and his family would *receive* salvation and be claimed by God as His. In choosing to belong to God, they would be made Family.

When Jericho's walls came down, a similar miracle occurred. Rahab (the prostitute who had hid the two spies) and her family were spared from death and brought into God's Family-nation (see Joshua 6:25). Time would prove Rahab's complete *acceptance*, despite her past, for she would become the wife of the Israelite Salmon and then the mother of Boaz, who would one day redeem and marry a woman named Ruth (see Ruth). Ruth, in being born a Moabite, would be banned by Law from ever becoming an Israelite (see Deuteronomy 23:3). Yet, by the grace of God's loving-goodness, Ruth would become the great-grandmother of King David, placing both Rahab and Ruth in Jesus' direct family line of earthly ancestry (see Matthew 1:5).

These women would honor God with respect and faith. In turn, they too would be honored. Their allegiance to God, His ways and His people would be evident in their faith that would show right respect of God, exalting Him from the heart. They wouldn't worship God with mere lip service, but with their lives.

> Do not be deceived: God cannot be mocked. A man reaps what he sows. (Galatians 6:7)

Unfortunately for the Israelites, after the Jericho victory, not every Israelite rightly honored God with respectful obedience. When God *gave* the Israelites instructions to devote all bounty to Him, their hearts were tested. All but one passed the test. Israelite Achan fell to temptation and *took* items that caught his eye. Rather shortsighted regarding God, he buried them in his tent.

In the meantime, a portion of the Israelite army moved on from Jericho to small town Ai, expecting to *take* it, too. But the tide turned against the Israelites, and they lost thirty-six men in a definitive routing. Heart-broken, the Israelites were confused. Where was God? Why had they been defeated?

When Joshua inquired of God, God revealed the reason. Sin was in the camp, and by Law, the nation suffered. Had the Israelites inquired of God before they had gone to Ai, they would have been *given* knowledge that would have spared lives. But they hadn't asked. Presumptuously, they had gone ahead of God (see Joshua 7). Then, to satisfy the Law and restore order, Achan and his family had to be stoned and then burned with their possessions. Only then could God lead the Israelites to further victory in *taking* Ai and cities beyond (see Joshua 8:1-29).

For centuries to come, throughout times that are now historical, the Israelites' failure to eliminate evil's presence from among them due to their lack of obedience to God would prove self-defeating time and again. One such occurrence would involve Haman, an Agagite who would persecute Jews in Persia during the time of Esther (see Esther 3). He would descend from Agag, the Amalekite king during King Saul's reign in Israel. The Amalekites had been an enemy of the Israelites since the Amalekites had ambushed them on their exodus journey from Egypt (see Exodus 17). Though God would later instruct King Saul in his God-*given* victory over the Amalekites to kill them all and *take* none of their possessions, Saul would instead spare life and *take* bounty at his own discretion (see 1 Samuel 15).

In choosing to defy God, King Saul would fail the test that would have promoted him into faith-filled victory. Instead, Saul would lose a personal battle with pride on a long downhill slide from honor. He would also set the stage for centuries of Israelite problems in dealing with remaining Amalekites. Had Saul honored God with obedience, he would have aided many.

The importance of annihilating all evil within their land was stressed by God via Moses to the Israelites even before they began to *take* their land. The instructions were explicit.

> When the LORD your God brings you into the land you are entering to possess and drives out before you many

nations---the Hitites, Girgashites, Amorites, Canaanites, Perizzites, Hivites and Jebusites, seven nations larger and stronger than you---and when the LORD your God has delivered them over to you and you have defeated them, then you must destroy them totally. Make no treaty with them, and show them no mercy. (Deuteronomy 7:1-2)

Do not be terrified by them, for the LORD your God, who is among you, is a great and awesome God. The LORD your God will drive out those nations before you little by little. You will not be allowed to eliminate them all at once, or the wild animals will multiply around you. But the LORD your God will deliver them over to you, throwing them into great confusion until they are destroyed. He will give their kings into your hand, and you will wipe out their names from under heaven. No one will be able to stand up against you; you will destroy them. The images of their gods you are to burn in the fire. Do not covet the silver and gold on them, and do not take it for yourselves, or you will be ensnared by it, for it is detestable to the LORD your God. Do not bring a detestable thing into your house or you, like it, will be set apart for destruction. Utterly abhor and detest it, for it is set apart for destruction. (Deuteronomy 7:21-26)

To love God, men must love what God loves and hate what God hates, for that which God hates is out to destroy that which He loves. When Jesus would allow Himself to be nailed to the Cross, the act would reflect love for Father and man, as well as intolerance for evil, which He would *take* to everlasting death. By *giving* men the opportunity they wanted to *take* Jesus' life, God would *give* men what they needed: opportunity to *receive* Jesus' life. Victory at every level is within a man's reach, if he is firmly positioned by God in Christ Jesus. To be so only requires affirmation of Truth, *giving* God an everlasting shout of praise.

"If God is for us, who can be against us?" (Romans 8:31b).

Far more than victorious, *God is Victory*... beginning to end, period.

# *The Standing* (The Kings)

**W**hile victory attained is glorious, victory retained can require ongoing intentional effort to keep it. Even when the Israelites *took* the territories from their enemies that God was *giving* them, their enemies rarely gave up trying to *take* the land back. The Amalekites weren't the only people who continued attacking the Israelites throughout their history. So did remnants of numerous other nations that Israel had defeated within its borders. In addition, other enemies have attacked Israel from the outside to enter in.

Israel has always stood apart from other nations of the world as being the home of God's covenant people. Considered to be an enemy by many nations who have stood opposed to the God of Abraham, Isaac and Jacob, Israel has often been targeted with hatred and warfare. Idol worshippers of various nationalities have wanted and tried to wipe Israel off the map since God first birthed His nation.

Even as Joshua and the Israelites were *taking* more of their God-*given* territory, coalescing it into the nation that God had outlined to Abraham, they were leaving a trail of defeated marauders within their expanding borders. When the majority of the Promised

Land was finally in the Israelites' possession and the twelve tribes were settling in their allotted portions (see Joshua 10-22), the battle to keep their inheritance began in earnest (see Joshua 13:13; 16:10; 23:7; Judges 1:1). Shortly before his death, Joshua spoke to Israel of the nation's continuing need to stand for God by standing with God. He knew that they couldn't afford to let their guard down and *give* evil license to dwell among them.

> The LORD has driven out before you great and powerful nations; to this day no one has been able to withstand you. One of you routs a thousand, because the LORD your God fights for you, just as he promised. So be very careful to love the LORD your God.
>
> But if you turn away and ally yourselves with the survivors of the nations that remain among you and if you intermarry with them and associate with them, then you may be sure that the LORD your God will no longer drive out these nations before you. Instead, they will become snares and traps for you, whips on your backs and thorns in your eyes, until you perish from this good land, which the LORD your God has given you. (Joshua 23:9-13)

God knew that the generation of Israelites who had *taken* Canaan was as equally proud of self-professed loyalty to God as had been their parents. So when Joshua's warning had little effect, Joshua spoke more forthrightly, detailing the limitation.

> Joshua said to the people, "You are not able to serve the LORD. He is a holy God; he is a jealous God. He will not forgive your rebellion and your sin. If you forsake the LORD and serve foreign gods, he will turn and bring disaster on you and make an end of you, after he has been good to you."

But the people said to Joshua, "No! We will serve the LORD." (Joshua 24:19-21)

So once again the Israelites entered into covenant with God, banking their futures on their ability to be faithful to Him (see Joshua 24:22-27). But after Joshua and all of the elders who had participated in *taking* Canaan died, the Israelites began to drift from God as Joshua had warned (see Joshua 24:28-31). What had been memories of God-*given* victories lost their edge when they became second and third-hand accounts to successive generations. Battles, it seemed, would have to be fought by each generation on more than one front.

During the forthcoming years, the Israelites' faith in God would continue to rhythmically rise and fall with the conditions of the times. When faith would decrease, enemies would advance against Israel. Then God would provide a leader---a judge---at just the right time and place to *give* Israel renewed faith that would lead to victory. Then, standing with God, the Israelites would watch their enemies fall. Pride would become an issue, faith would falter and enemies would advance, leading to the next judge being positioned by God.

Each judge was *given* specific time and battle. Caleb's younger brother, Othniel, delivered the Israelites from eight years of subjection to enemy Cushan-Rishathaim (see Judges 3:7-11). Ehud killed the King of Moab to defeat the combined forces of the

Moabites, Ammonites and Amalekites (see Judges 3:12-30). Deborah, a prophetess judge, led Barak in defeating the commander of King Jabin's Canaanite army (see Judges 4-5). Samson, despite his battle with pride, freed the nation from the Philistines (see Judges 13-16). Other judges each did their part, honoring God by standing with Him against enemy nations.

But despite the victories that the Israelites were *given*, enabling them to continue living in their land of plenty, they were not satisfied. They still wanted "more." This time they wanted a king, as other nations had. The one nation on the Earth that God had claimed as His was jealous of godless enemies who had mortal kings (see 1 Samuel 8). So God *gave* them the king that they wanted in order to *give* them what they needed: opportunity to learn firsthand that no man from their own ranks could ever be the kind of king that they really needed.

In due time, Jesus would be revealed to be eternal "KING OF KINGS AND LORD OF LORDS" (Revelation 19:16b). He would lead mankind into His honor and glory by conquering their greatest enemies, sin and death, for them. His steadfast stand with God the Father in Holy Spirit guidance would be far more honorable than any earthly king's ever could be.

But first God had to shed light on men's thinking with regard to their limited ability to rightly rule one another. He did so by *giving* the job of anointing Israel's first king to Samuel, Israel's final judge. God consoled Samuel with the Truth.

And the LORD told him: "Listen to all that the people are saying to you; it is not you they have rejected, but they have rejected me as their king. As they have done from the day I brought them up out of Egypt until this day, forsaking me and serving other gods, so they are doing to you." (1 Samuel 8:7-8)

Samuel stood with God by anointing Saul, the man whom God had hand-picked to be Israel's first king (see 1 Samuel 9-12). Saul was "an impressive young man without equal among the Israelites---a head taller than any of the others" (1 Samuel 9:2b). Saul's daunting stature *gave* him a kingly look by men's limited standards of measurement.

But a good appearance does not a good leader make. Being a good follower of God does, and Saul failed miserably on that account. Departing from God's ways, Saul was a terrible king. His temper often raged from selfish concerns, serving Saul's pride alone and dishonoring both God and the men for whom Saul was supposed to care. Saul failed to live up to both his appearance and men's expectations (see 1 Samuel 15).

Why then did God choose to make Saul, of all men, king? As always, God acted in man's best interest. The only way to eliminate the pride over which men continually stumble, distancing them from God, is for pride to play itself out to failure. Humble submission to God's right ways only follows pride coming to its own dead end.

By having Samuel anoint Saul's successor fairly early in Saul's reign, God let it be known that Saul's days as king were numbered. The throne would not go to a son of Saul, as men would consider natural, but to a man chosen by God, who always knows what men need. The man God anointed was not even yet a man, but was still a boy---a boy after God's own heart (see 1 Samuel 13:14; Acts 13:22). The boy was David, the shepherd boy who would become a legendary hero after slaying Goliath and be called a good man by men whose judgment lacked much relative to that of God (see 1 Samuel 17-18).

David was different from Saul in both appearance and demeanor. Young when anointed, David had time to grow into the position under God's hand before being made king. As the youngest of eight sons, David's family often discounted him. When his father, Jesse, had his other sons pass before Samuel in the selection process for king, David was left out. He was literally left out in the fields to tend the family's sheep... until Samuel specifically inquired as to whether or not Jesse had any additional sons than the seven before him (see 1 Samuel 16).

But even after Samuel anointed David as future king, David's brothers failed to hold him in high regard. When David was sent by his father to deliver lunch to his brothers at the battlefield where he found Goliath intimidating the entire Israelite army, David's oldest brother chastised David's inquiry regarding the king's reward for defeating Goliath. When David's brother told him that he should have stayed home with the sheep, David simply stood his ground. He didn't argue; he didn't debate. Instead, David *took* a stance for God against the real enemy: Goliath, the uncircumcised Philistine who mocked God. David knew which battles were important to fight and which ones were not. In fighting Goliath, but not his brother, David *received* honor by honoring right over wrong (see 1 Samuel 17).

There would come a time in Jesus' life when He, too, would be chastised by His family: "For even his own brothers did not believe in him" (John 7:5). Jesus, though, would not *take* offense at His family's remarks that would be less than honoring of Him. Rather, He would expand the concept of family, making it more inclusionary: "For whoever does the will of my Father in heaven is my brother and sister and mother" (Matthew 12:50). Jesus would not fight against His earthly family, but for God's Family.

Though David's birth family showed him little respect at times, his blood covenant brother, Jonathan, always did (see 1 Samuel 20). Jonathan was Saul's son, but he did not have his father's prideful temperament. He and David served each other, God and their nation well in love by honoring their covenant.

Even when King Saul attempted to hatefully murder David (see 1 Samuel 18:5-20:42), David twice refused to take Saul's life when he was *given* opportunity. David passed the honor test, honoring not Saul, but God's anointing on Saul that had made Saul king (see 1 Samuel 24, 26).

David also honored God when he *accepted* correction from Abigail, the wife of Nabal, a man who had wronged David. David's decision to repent of his sinful intention changed his course of action from wrong to right. Thereby, David rightly glorified God by forgoing trying to glorify himself (see 1 Samuel 25).

But as good and as honorable as some of David's decisions were, he did not always live right, for no man but Jesus ever would. An infamous segment of David's life was filled with dishonorable decisions that broke most, if not all, of the Ten Commandments (see 2 Samuel 11-12). David not only coveted, but also *took* Bathsheba, the wife of his friend Uriah, to satisfy his desire. Then, instead of repenting, he sinned further. Attempting to hide his adulterous acts, he lied to and deceived Uriah all of the way to Uriah's murder on a battlefield of betrayal on which Uriah wasn't even aware that he was fighting.

How could a man with a heart for God have acted so reprehensibly? The answer lies in the fact that David was a man *after* God's heart, not *with* God's heart, and the difference is important. As much as any man, even beloved David, would try to be good, in essence to be as good as God, no man but the Son of God could be. David failed the perfection test and fell to temptation, as all men do. The event did not surprise God, who, even in having known of David's sin with Bathsheba before it occurred, still had Nathan, the Prophet, promise David an everlasting familial reign. A good and loving God remained steadfastly honorable by acting in the best interest of all men, despite their ongoing sin against Him and one another.

The LORD declares to you that the LORD himself will establish a house for you ... Your house and your kingdom will endure forever before me; your throne will be established forever. (2 Samuel 7:11b, 16)

The promise would one day be fulfilled in Jesus, whose earthly ancestral lines would pass through David and Bathsheba on their way to Mary and Joseph, Jesus' parents in this world (see Luke 3:31-32; Matthew 1:6). The fact of the matter is that, in God's eyes, every person on Jesus' family tree would be as equally sinful as were David and Bathsheba. The sins of Jesus' other ancestors just weren't all recorded for men's general knowledge. Once Adam had sinned, all men became infected through Adam's seed. No one would be immune except Jesus, who would inherit His Father's righteousness instead of man's sin.

David's personal restoration, *given* to him by the grace of God, came through David's eventual repentance when he was confronted by Nathan with the Truth. Unlike Saul's self-justification that further dishonored God and Saul, David's confession of guilt dignified David by honoring Truth and God.

Then David said to Nathan, "I have sinned against the LORD."

Nathan replied, "The LORD has taken away your sin. You are not going to die. But because by doing this you have made the enemies of the LORD show utter contempt, the son born to you will die." (2 Samuel 12:13-14)

Sin has consequences, and David's sin was no exception. But still, how could a good and loving God *take* the life of an innocent child in payment for David's sin? How could God make a son pay?

As adorably precious as babies are, they are not sinless (see Psalm 51:5). In descending from Adam, they are born into mankind's separated state from God, inheriting sin (a noun). Then, as sinners, they too begin to sin (a verb) as they grow in that state.

When the Law needed a death to balance the justice scales, David's son paid the bill, as Pharaoh's son had once paid for Pharaoh's contempt for God in Egypt, for sin's effects were generational. Though David prayed for his son to live, he *accepted* the death as righteous before God by Law. David understood as best as he could, and God understood completely. Long before either David or his son were born, God knew full well the suffering of the father and the son in the knowledge of His own Son's death that would one day pay for all men's sin.

God kept His Word, as always, and passed the throne to Solomon, the next son born to David and Bathsheba. Before David died, he did his best to assure a smooth transition in leadership by having Solomon anointed, not by one man, but by three: Zadok--- priest; Nathan---prophet; and Benaiah---a Mighty Men general (see 1 Kings 1:28-2:46). With the three acting in agreement with God's words under David's direction, Solomon's ascension was uncontested.

Initially, Solomon followed in his father's footsteps, honoring God foremost. Humbly, he sought wisdom from God (see

1 Kings 3). Then he built the Temple (see 1 Kings 5-8) upon the threshing floor that David had purchased for men's worship of God (see 2 Samuel 24:18-25). But even amid his much amassed wealth, Solomon wasn't content (see 1 Kings 9:10-10:29). He wasn't wise enough to realize that only God fully satisfies.

> I denied myself nothing my eyes desired; I refused my heart no pleasure. My heart took delight in all my work, and this was the reward for all my labor. Yet when I had surveyed all that my hands had done and what I had toiled to achieve, everything was meaningless, a chasing after the wind; nothing was gained under the sun. (Ecclesiastes 2:10-11)

In wanting yet "more," Solomon focused most unwisely on what he wanted most: foreign women, whom he brought, along with their idol worship, into his land and his home. Temptation succeeded in multiplying Solomon's wives and concubines to the exorbitant numbers of seven hundred and three hundred, respectively (see 1 Kings 11:3). With lust *given* precedence over honor, Solomon's reign did not end well.

> As Solomon grew old, his wives turned his heart after other gods, and his heart was not fully devoted to the LORD his God, as the heart of David his father had been. (1 Kings 11:4)

The less that Solomon honored God, the more that discord *took* hold in his family and his nation, tearing both apart. Idol worship, through self-worship that failed to rightly worship God, brought division. The nation split in two, pitting brother against brother. The ten northern tribes united as the Kingdom of Israel (also known as Ephraim---Joshua's tribe). The two southern tribes of Judah and Benjamin united as the Kingdom of Judah (Caleb's tribe) and possessed the Temple in Jerusalem (see 1 Kings 11:32).

In actuality, two half tribes from Joseph's sons made thirteen total tribes (Joshua 17:17-18); Simeon was located within Judah's borders (Joshua 19:9), and Levites had no land of their own (Deuteronomy 18:1). Logistically, the split was nine/three.

From this time on, Judah's inhabitants were known as Jews. Eventually Samaria became the northern kingdom's capital and high place of worship, and its people incorporated with others into a blended nationality and faith (see 1 Kings 16). Hence, Samaritans were not viewed honorably by Jews.

Through the coming years, both kingdoms failed to consistently honor God rightly. Worship of God waxed and waned with the reigns of alternating good and bad kings, who led their kingdoms first in one direction and then in another. By not standing firmly with God, both kingdoms made themselves vulnerable to the attacks of other nations. In time, the northern kingdom fell to Assyria (see 2 Kings 17), and the southern kingdom fell to Babylon (see 2 Kings 24-25). Many people from both kingdoms were *taken* from their God-*given* homes into exile in foreign idol-worshipping lands in exchange for foreigners who then inhabited their land.

The day would come when Jesus would declare, "Every kingdom divided against itself will be ruined, and every city or household divided against itself will not stand" (Matthew 12:25; see also Mark 3:25; Luke 11:17). Jesus would recognize that infighting is a ploy of evil that usurps strength to prevent the standing of a strong united front. Strife aids and abets the enemy, preventing peace. It is often the result of men being more concerned with their standing among men than with their standing with God (see Galatians 1:10). When men fight a battle with each other that they should be fighting against evil, they fight the enemy's battle for him, his way, dishonoring God.

One day, Jesus would purposefully go through Samaria on His way to Galilee from Judea. One reason for doing so would be to restore honor to a socially outcast Samaritan woman. Having had five previous husbands, the woman would then be living with yet another man who was not her husband. To avoid seeing her shame reflected in the eyes of other women, she would go to the well alone in the hot noonday sun to fetch the water that she needed to survive. There one day, Jesus---a Jewish male---would be waiting to openly converse with her---a sinful Samaritan woman. With three strikes of gender, nationality and religion against her, the woman would be counted down and out by many; but not so by Jesus. He would count His Father's way. To God, every individual is of number one importance.

So as God had once removed the reproach of Egypt from the Israelites, marking personal identification with Him through circumcision, Jesus would similarly *give* the woman at the well personal identification with God through her relationship with Him. The honor of having Jesus reveal significant information about

Himself to her would trump the shame of her past, *giving* her a respected future that would include sharing the Good News of Jesus with others. In *accepting* Jesus as Messiah, she herself would *receive* everlasting *acceptance* (see John 4:1-42).

The day would come when Jesus would *take* all men's sin and shame upon Himself (see Hebrews 12:2) and share His dignity with all who would consider *accepting* Him as Savior to be an honor. His *acceptance* of them in the midst of their many outcast conditions would *give* them each an honorable future (see Romans 8:1).

The pride of a man in thinking too little of himself can be as equally detrimental to his relationship with God as can be his thinking too much of himself. Both views distort the Truth in disagreement with God. In order for a man to stand with God, he must *accept* Jesus' *acceptance* of him as righteous before God.

A woman suffering abnormal bleeding for twelve years would one day make her way to Jesus through a thronging crowd (see Matthew 9:20-22; Mark 5:24b-34; Luke 8:42b-48). At some time, from someone, she would hear something that would make her think that Jesus was the solution to her problem.

For the most part, this woman, ruled unclean by the Law, would be essentially housebound and confined to her mat, for everywhere she would sit or lie would become unclean. Anyone who would touch her or those places would also become unclean and have to go through a lengthy cleansing process before resuming a normal life (see Leviticus 15:25-27). This woman would not only be sick, tired and out of funds, but she would also be a nuisance to be around. Even in her home she would be socially outcast, unable to participate in many family events.

But then she would hear about Jesus and the miracles that He would do in restoring lives to wholeness. How much she would hear or the period of time over which she would hear it, the Bible does not record. But the hearing would be sufficient to cause her to put aside the shame of her suffering to venture forth, touching people against the Law and expecting the grace of God's power in Jesus to heal her. The revelation that would send her out to touch Jesus would lead to personal experience with Him that would change not only her physical condition, but also her identity. After twelve years of being known as "the woman with the issue of blood," she would become "the woman who was healed by touching Jesus." Her right expectation of Jesus that would honor Him would lead to Jesus honoring her for having faith that would stand out in a crowd. Honor mattered.

The nation of Israel only had three kings, and none proved to be truly honorable. One had good looks, one had a good heart and one had a good mind. One's strength was in his physical being, and the others' were in parts of their souls. But not one of them had all that was needed to stand honorably before God all of the time, let alone lead other men to do so.

Only Jesus would meet men's need for perfection, for even while living in a body, He would be ruled by the heart, mind and Spirit of God. Though David tried to do right, Solomon wanted to do right and Saul both wanted and tried to make his own way right, Jesus would just be right. Anointed as Prophet, Priest and Military Leader by His Father, Jesus would stand without question as eternal King, worthy of all honoring.

Far more than honorable, *God is Honor*... beginning to end, period.

# *The Revealing* (John the Baptist)

Jesus. The Name says it All. But the people of Judea (Roman occupied Judah) and Galilee wouldn't know that when they would first see Jesus coming into their towns and into their lives to turn their worlds upside down. Though the Magi (see Matthew 2:1-12), Simeon and Anna (see Luke 2:21-38) would recognize Jesus as Savior early in His life, few others would. His identity as the Son of God, the One who would reveal His Father to the world, would not be formally announced until the baptismal launching of His ministry at the age of thirty.

Prior to Jesus' birth, during the times of kings, wars and exiles, God's Prophets regularly *gave* the people hope in the foretelling of a coming Messiah (Savior). The Promised One, they said, would lead God's people out of oppression and into freedom. As their King, He would *give* them victory in defeat of their enemies. But the Prophets never disclosed when Messiah was coming, only that He was coming. So each generation watched and waited, hoping that their time would be His time.

But there came a time when all prophecies stopped. For four hundred years, silence alone was heard from God. During that time, the Jews *received* no new Prophets or words. So the people continued searching the words that they had, looking for clues regarding their coming deliverance. With an increasing hunger and thirst for righteousness, they wanted relief from the oppression of their enemies. But even greater than their need for freedom from unjust nations was their need for deliverance from the unjustness of their own wrong thinking that prevented them from recognizing their own true need (see John 8:31-41).

While the Jews waited out the silence, the Law remained in effect, and the Temple remained the hub of religious life. But over that span of time, the Law continued to be further interpreted by men who stacked up more *do* and *don't* rules in attempted clarifications that became additional traditions. Men regularly spun God's perfect Law to fit their own thinking.

So even while the Law was being enforced, it was also being stretched in directions that it was never intended to go. Extrapolations increased freedom in some ways and decreased it in others. Though the Law itself remained black and white, life by its letter instead of its heart became a gray legalistic mixture of God's Law and men's. Men's personal interpretations of the Law that defined right living only further increased the list of sins that men could look for in one another. Additional differentiations between individuals produced greater strife and division among men who were supposed to be living in unison. They forgot that God alone is the Righteous One (see Jeremiah 23:6).

The mixture caused an overall digression in relationships that, as Jesus would reveal, lacked mercy and compassion, thereby further isolating individuals in a general lack of *acceptance*. Jesus would also reveal Himself to be the only One capable of disentangling the wrong thinking that produced the mixture in the first place, thereby binding men back together.

Jesus would be anything but the kind of Messiah for whom the people were looking. Being so much more than their expectations, the reality of Jesus would be difficult to *accept* by those individuals who would refuse to open their minds to the new possibilities that Jesus' Presence would offer.

So once again, God chose to use a man to guide men in the way they should go. This time the man selected was John the Baptist, a cousin of Jesus. The direction in which John was to lead men was in terms of their thinking. John would be the "lamp" (John 5:35) pointing to Jesus, who would, in turn, light the way to God, revealing the Truth of God's loving-goodness towards all men. Jesus would be perfect interpretation of the Law as God intended for the Law to be lived: with God's heart.

John the Baptist was the last of the Prophets, and he left no doubt about his identity, stating "I am the voice of the one calling in the desert, 'Make straight the way for the Lord'" (John 1:23). John's voice broke the four hundred year drought of silence from God with a one word directive---*repent*. The word said a lot to men who had little right understanding of God.

> And so John came, baptizing in the desert region and preaching a baptism of repentance for the forgiveness of sins. The whole Judean countryside and all the people of

Jerusalem went out to him. Confessing their sins, they were baptized by him in the Jordan River. John wore clothing made of camel's hair with a leather belt around his waist, and he ate locust and wild honey. And this was his message: After me will come one more powerful than I, the thongs of whose sandals I am not worthy to stoop down and untie. I baptize you with water, but he will baptize you with the Holy Spirit. (Mark 1:4-8)

John baptized (immersed) repentant individuals in water. By Law, washings were important purification rituals that applied at times to priests, sacrificed animals, clothes, pots and other items (see Numbers 19). John's baptism, however, was preparing men to *receive* a new kind of cleansing from Jesus.

God was doing a "new thing" (Isaiah 43:19) through John, and people were flocking to him (see Matthew 3:1-17; Mark 1:1-11; Luke 3:1-20; John 1:19-34). So hungry were they for words from God that they came from near and far to hear what a man living humbly in a remote location outside of Jerusalem had to say.

Those who listened to John and were baptized by him in the Jordan (the river that had been crossed to *take* Canaan) *accepted* important components of God's salvation package that Jesus would deliver. John's life was used by God to prepare men to *accept* right thinking that would save them from the coming wrath of God due sin. John described to varying individuals how personal repentance should be lived.

"What should we do then?" the crowd asked.

John answered, "The man with two tunics should share with him who has none, and the one who has food should do the same."

Tax collectors also came to be baptized. "Teacher," they asked, "what should we do?"

"Don't collect any more than you are required to," he told them.

Then some soldiers asked him, "And what should we do?"

He replied, "Don't extort money and don't accuse people falsely--be content with your pay." (Luke 3:10-14b)

John revealed that repentance is personal. It occurs in the realigning of a man's heart and mind to the heart and mind of God in a unique way that is between him and God. Collectively, repentance unites men, as each one is shifted by God into greater uniformity with Him, bringing them closer to one another.

Not everyone, though, who heard John's message of repentance, appreciated its application to their personal lives. When John revealed to Herod the tetrarch (a puppet leader who was a Jew in name only) that repentance for Herod would mean that he would have to stop living with his brother's wife, ire against John flared within Herod's household. Eventually, John's boldness in speaking Truth to Herod would cost John his mortal life (See Luke 3:19-20; Matthew 14:1-12), for not all men would be willing to *give* up self-righteous thinking.

There came a day in John's life when Jesus proclaimed that "among those born of women, there is no one greater than John"

(Luke 7:28a; see also Matthew 11:11). Yet John would be beheaded by Herod for speaking words that God *gave* to him to speak. When Herod imprisoned John, Jesus did not extricate John, who was family, friend and Prophet of God. Why not? How could Jesus have left John imprisoned to die?

John's life, precious to God, was used by God to pave the way for all men, including John, to *receive* everlasting freedom in Christ Jesus. The freedom provided would be freedom from sin and its subsequent death sentence to hell that would otherwise imprison all men's souls with it forever. God used John's wrongful death at the hands of Herod in the same way that He used John's life: to pave the way to salvation.

When John's disciples questioned the ministry of Jesus, relative to that of John, John declared, "He must become greater; I must become less" (John 3:30). The reason would be *given* by Jesus, who would say, "For all the Prophets and the Law prophesied until John" (Matthew 11:13). Not only did John the Baptist's life herald in the new, his death also began ushering out the old. John's time was a time of transition. Once Jesus would die, fulfilling the Law, and then resurrect, *giving* men everlasting life, the Law which John represented would be obsolete. A new and greater covenant would be in effect (see Hebrews 8:13).

Grace, freely *given,* and the Law, accomplished by works, would not mix. Each man would have to choose to live by one or the other, determining to live a future either with Jesus or without Him. Those who would depend upon the self-righteousness of their own good works would be judged unrighteous by Law, as they must be for their sinfulness. But those who would put their faith in the righteousness of Jesus would be judged righteous in Him by God's good and loving gift of merciful grace.

> Now we know that whatever the law says, it says to those who are under the law, so that every mouth may be silenced and the whole world held accountable to God. Therefore no one will be declared righteous in his sight by observing the law; rather, through the law we become conscious of sin.
>
> But now a righteousness from God, apart from law, has been made known, to which the Law and the Prophets testify. This righteousness from God comes through faith in Jesus Christ to all who believe. (Romans 3:19-22a)

John's time necessarily overlapped with that of Jesus, but it had to end with the ramping up of the establishment of the new covenant in Christ. As gruesome as John's beheading was, it was an honorable, though unjust, death that is recognized in heaven for its *acceptance* by John in his refusal to back down from speaking the Truth. John was but one of many men who either have walked or yet will walk the same path, forfeiting the temporal for the everlasting. In Apostle John's later vision of Revelation, God would reveal end time honor that is to be *given* to all who will be beheaded for not denying Jesus as Lord.

> I saw thrones on which were seated those who had been given authority to judge. And I saw the souls of those who had been beheaded because of their testimony for Jesus and because of the word of God. They had not worshiped the beast or his image and had not received his mark on their

foreheads. They came to life and reigned with Christ a thousand years. (Revelation 20:4)

But first, John the Baptist was to be honored by God in this world with the opportunity to baptize Jesus. The honor included John being *given* testimony of Jesus that he would then be honored to freely *give* to the world.

> I saw the Spirit come down from heaven as a dove and remain on him. I would not have known him, except that the one who sent me to baptize with water told me, "The man on whom you see the Spirit come down and remain is he who will baptize with the Holy Spirit." I have seen and I testify that this is the Son of God. (John 1:32-34)

John's testimony followed his personal experience with the Truth as God had revealed it to him. In testifying to the identity of Jesus, John simultaneously testified to the Truth of God's words and, therefore, to the Truth of God. The testimonies were interwoven and inseparable, for Jesus is the living Word of God (see John 1:1), *given* to reveal the Truth to all men through personal experience that becomes testimony.

As men heard John's testimony and opened their minds to the possibility of its Truth, they began *accepting* Jesus' open invitation to follow Him. In doing so, they would hear and experience Truth personally. One question above all others would lead them to follow Jesus: Was Jesus indeed the Messiah?

Some who would follow Jesus would become His true disciples, fully *accepting* the Truth that they would learn from Him. As such, they themselves would be made witnesses by God. In testifying, they would enlarge the circles of those who would hear the Truth and those who would *accept* it (see John 1:35-51). Then new followers and disciples would again begin the cycle in endless testimony of the Truth of God.

Once Jesus was revealed by His Father during His baptism and then affirmed by John's testimony, He would no longer be a secret. The Good News about Jesus would flow out from wherever He was to reach new areas before He did. Crowds would come in search of answers that no one else had, leaving Jesus precious little time to be alone in prayer with His Father. He would seek that private time whenever possible, for it alone would meet His need (see Mark 1:35; Luke 6:12). Even when Jesus would *receive* news of John the Baptist's death, the many needs of the people would *give* him little time to be alone.

> John's disciples came and took his body and buried it. Then they went and told Jesus. When Jesus heard what had happened, he withdrew by boat privately to a solitary place. Hearing this, the crowds followed him on foot from the towns. When Jesus landed and saw a large crowd, he had compassion on them and healed their sick. (Matthew 14:12-14)

Every aspect of Jesus' life would be used for the welfare of others. His every word and deed would reveal the Truth of a good and loving God to men whose concept of good and loving lacked the substance of goodness and love that filled Jesus. Those who would *accept* Jesus' ways as right before God would open their hearts and minds to *take* His way of life as their own, absorbing His every word. Doing so would benefit them in reverberation of their lives benefitting others. But those who would deny themselves the opportunity to change in accordance with Jesus would forfeit much in this life and/or the next.

The message of repentance that God *gave* to John the Baptist to share with men was God's plea to mankind to *receive* the saving grace of Truth that Jesus would come offering to all men. In order for anyone to *receive* it, though, they would have to be open to having their understanding of Truth made right by Jesus, who Himself was an open book. As Apostle John would write, "... grace and truth came through Jesus Christ. No one has ever seen God, but God the One and Only, who is at the Father's side, has made him known" (John 1:17b-18).

The concept of men seeing and coming to know God by looking at and knowing a man---Jesus---would be difficult for men in general to *accept*. As late as the Last Supper, just prior to Jesus' crucifixion, Jesus' closest disciples would still be grappling with the concept.

> Philip said, "Lord, show us the Father and that will be enough for us."
>
> Jesus answered: "Don't you know me, Philip, even after I have been among you such a long time? Anyone who has

seen me has seen the Father. How can you say, 'Show us the Father?'" (John 14:8-9)

That same evening, Jesus would pray a lengthy prayer in the presence of His disciples, acknowledging His Oneness with God the Father. He would pray for that same Oneness to be the reality of His disciples, as well as all who would come to believe in Him through them (see John 17:5-26). His prayer would be to God's glory.

> Father, the time has come. Glorify your Son, that your Son may glorify you. For you granted him authority over all people that he might give eternal life to all those you have given him. Now this is eternal life: that they may know you, the only true God, and Jesus Christ, whom you have sent ...
>
> I have revealed you to those whom you gave me out of the world. They were yours; you gave them to me and they have obeyed your word. Now they know that everything that you have given me comes from you. For I gave them the words you gave me and they accepted them ...
>
> I have given them the glory that you gave me, that they may be one as we are one: I in them and you in me. May they be brought to complete unity to let the world know that you sent me and have loved them even as you have loved me ...
>
> I have made you known to them, and will continue to make you known in order that the love you have for me may be in them and that I myself may be in them. (John 17:1-3, 6-8a, 22-23, 26)

All who would come to *accept* Jesus Christ as Savior would *receive* everlasting *acceptance* in Him to be made One with God. By the Law's *acceptance* of Jesus as righteous, God would have the right to *accept* by grace all who would *take* refuge in Jesus.

Though on a much grander scale than as had occurred in the days of Noah, a Family would be saved by faith in God's grace. All who would *accept* a free pass from God to get onboard with His salvation plan would live. By *accepting* Jesus' offer to ride out the storm safely in Him, no man would ever need to fear God's wrath due sin. God's salvation plan is a Family plan. Once onboard, a son is a son forever (see John 8:35).

Far more than accepting, *God is Acceptance...* beginning to end, period.

# *The Ministering* (Jesus Christ)

One: one man, one job. One man at a time is all God has ever needed to get a job done. Throughout all of time, each man has come and gone in his own set time, living out the time assigned to him, either his way or God's way. Still lined up in time's continuum are more men whose specified times await them, for God has ordained since before time's beginning that their times will indeed come. At God's discretion, time moves on, for it is still not yet complete.

But the finished work of the Cross is: "It is finished" (John 19:30a). The work was completed by the One Man alone who was capable of delivering salvation. Jesus stepped into His God-appointed time, as God's One and Only Man for the job.

Jesus fulfilled every one of more than three hundred prophecies from God that were ever spoken about Him. He was not a statistical fluke of nature, for He came from beyond the realms of both statistical probability and physical laws. Neither was He merely a good man and teacher, but rather the Messiah/Savior, King and so much more.

For the most part, Jesus allowed others around Him to deduce His identity from His life. But in the end, when He was asked directly, He confirmed the Truth. To Pilate, the governor who represented the Roman Emperor and oversaw local politics through King Herod, Jesus admitted during His trial to being a King of a different kind. His confession was specific for that time and place, for Pilate was a Gentile concerned with the governing authority of men in this world.

> Jesus said, "My kingdom is not of this world. If it were, my servants would fight to prevent my arrest by the Jews. But now my kingdom is from another place." (John 18:36)

To the chief priests and the teachers of the Law, Jesus made a different confession, for they were Jews concerned about the rule of God's Kingdom. To them, He admitted to being the Son of God, whose rule is forever.

> "If you are the Christ," they said, "tell us."
>
> Jesus answered, "If I tell you, you will not believe me; and if I asked you, you would not answer. But from now on, the Son of Man will be seated at the right hand of the mighty God."
>
> They all asked, "Are you then the Son of God?"
>
> He replied, "You are right in saying I am." (Luke 22:67-70)

While men debated Jesus' identity, most acknowledged that He was Rabbi: teacher. That title was endorsed by many, including Judas Iscariot---the man who would betray Jesus to His opponents with a kiss (see Matthew 26:48-49). Even at the Last Supper, when the other disciples would address Jesus as Lord, Judas would simply call Him Rabbi, no more (see Matthew 26:20-25). But if Rabbi was all that Jesus was, then He could not have been a good one. For if He were not also the Son of God and King, as He so claimed to be, then He would have been a liar, which is not an attribute of any good teacher. Had Jesus lied even once, His every word would be suspect.

But Jesus was indeed a good teacher in every sense, and as such, He left His personal mark on the world, as other teachers have also left theirs, albeit to lesser degrees. But once dead and buried, the others have remained dead. But Jesus would walk out of His grave to mark eternity with the nail holes that He would bear on His Body, making Him Lord of all, even death.

> Christ died and returned to life so that he might be the Lord of both the dead and the living. (Romans 14:9)

Walking among as many as five hundred people at a time after His Resurrection (see 1 Corinthians 15:3-8), Jesus would make witnesses of all who would see Him. The witnesses would share their testimonies with others, spreading the Good News: "He has risen!" (Mark 16:6c; Luke 24:6b). Had Jesus not risen, men's hope in Him would be futile, no different than misplaced hope in any other man (see 1 Corinthians 15:12-28).

But Jesus did indeed rise, proving that He was not simply a good man to be emulated in this world, but that He was the Perfect Man, who cannot be equaled. His perfection was and will always be complete in every way. Being the exact image of His Father, Jesus revealed God's loving-goodness to the world as no sinful man ever could. The entirety of Jesus' life remained right on target with His Father's will, for Jesus was the One "who gave himself for our sins to rescue us from the present evil age, according to the will of our God and Father" (Galatians 1:4).

Though fully man, Jesus was also fully God. He spoke of His timelessness to the Jews, saying "... before Abraham was, I am" (John 8:58b). At a later time, He told His disciples of His coming betrayal in advance "so that when it does happen you will believe that I am He" (John 13:19b).

The word *He* in the preceding verse was added by translators, who likewise added it to other verses, also (see John 4:26, 8:24, 8:28, 18:5, 18:6, 18:8). In each of these instances, the Greek verb, translating as *I am* is one and the same verb, indicative of present tense. Likewise, the same Greek verb and tense were used in Luke 22:70 (above) when Jesus said, "You are right in saying I am." Noteworthy, also, is that when Jesus said, "I am" in John 18:6, everyone who was present to arrest Him fell to the ground.

Jesus' use of *I am* has special significance. Though the Old Testament is recorded in Hebrew, Jesus' words make reference to God's Self-identification to Moses at the burning bush when God said, "I AM WHO I AM" (Exodus 3:14a). Jesus also used the same present tense form in His *I am* statements: "I am the gate" (John 10:7, 9), "I am the resurrection and the life" (John 11:25), etc. (see John 6:48, 8:12, 10:11, 14:6, 15:5 for others). Being God, Jesus lives forever in the present. Being eternal, He is timeless.

Therefore, Jesus' statements about Himself also revealed unchanging eternal qualities of His Father. Thereby, the Father was seen through Jesus, for Jesus was the physical manifestation of God on earth. "The Son is the radiance of God's glory and the exact representation of his being, sustaining all things by his powerful word" (Hebrews 1:3a). With Jesus' every word and act important in revealing the grace and Truth of God the Father, everything that has been recorded about Jesus is significant... *everything*.

When a man with leprosy (a deadly, contagious disease that ostracized victims) knelt before Jesus, the man begged, "If you are willing, you can make me clean" (Mark 1:40b). Jesus could have done any number of things at that moment, including healing the man's body and going on His way. But like His Father, whose loving-goodness is abundant, He chose to do so much more than that which the man had dared to hope.

Seeing and hearing the man's unvoiced need that equaled or surpassed his need for physical healing, Jesus did the completely unexpected. According to both the Law and worldly logic, Jesus should have kept His distance from the leper, as did everyone else, keeping the man isolated. But He didn't. He did the opposite of what was expected and what the Law precluded. In doing so, He undoubtedly dazed all who were present to witness God's love for the man in action.

> Filled with compassion, Jesus reached out and touched the man. (Mark 1:41a)

Jesus touched him! Jesus purposefully touched a leper:  a man whose deformity increased daily and was passed from man to man by physical contact. While the man's body was growing number each day, his soul was experiencing greater pain with each passing moment. The man, rejected by others because of his uncleanness, was hurt inside and out. His outward condition signaled a heart-deep one to Jesus, who *gave* first priority not to the man's body, but to his wholeness.

Jesus' touch reached inside the man's body and touched the man's soul. Jesus' righteousness more than compensated for the man's brokenness. Whereas the Law declared that touching anything unclean defiles a man (see Leviticus 13), the touch of Jesus said, in effect, "Look again. Righteousness is the greater." Righteousness, coming only from God, proved to be far more powerfully contagious than any defilement. Like water flowing downstream, the life that filled Jesus in His right standing with the Father flowed from Jesus' higher potential to the lower one in the leper, filling the man's need.

The touch from Jesus *gave* the man what he needed most: tangible love that *accepted* him as he was, independent of his condition. It proved to the man and to others that the man was not untouchable, but was greatly loved, for not even the man's family members would have been willing to have touched him as Jesus did. The touch said, "You are important. You matter." Only after Jesus had settled the man's heart and mind with a touch did He then restore the man's body with a word, rightly prioritizing the man's healing according to his total need.

> "I am willing," [Jesus[ said. "Be clean!" Immediately the leprosy left him and he was cured. (Mark 1:41b-42)

The word *cured* indicates that purification from the ailment had occurred. Purification—the removal of qualities apart from those connected to God—is of primary importance to restoring intimate fellowship between Holy God and sinful men. David, in his day, cried out for purification, saying, "Wash away all my iniquity and cleanse me of my sin" (Psalm 51:2). Upon the Cross, the Lord Jesus would meet the need (see Hebrews 1:3)

> For [the LORD] will be like a refiner's fire or a launderer's soap. He will sit as a refiner and a purifier of silver; he will purify the Levites and refine them like gold and silver. Then the LORD will have men who will bring offerings in righteousness ... (Malachi 3:2c-3)

Jesus, the Living Word of God Almighty, cleanses men's thoughts from the defilement of wrong thinking with His words of Truth. On the night before His death, Jesus would tell His disciples, who would have been studying Jesus up close and personal for more than three years by then, "You are already clean because of the word I have spoken to you" (John 15:3).

But men needed even more than "the washing with water through the word" (Ephesians 5:26), which is why Jesus didn't stop short of action that *gave* completion to His words. Men needed to be forgiven. They needed to be purged of residential sin and have the records of their association with sin permanently expunged, leaving their souls free from sin's contamination---past, present and future. Then, no longer set apart *from* God by sin, they would be set apart *for* God forever. The purity of Jesus' righteousness would be the cleansing agent that would dissolve sin's stain in men, *giving* forgiveness in a way that no one had ever expected.

Also unexpected was the preview that Jesus *gave* one day of the forgiveness that was to come. Four men, desperately trying to deliver their paralytic friend to Jesus, dug a hole through the roof of the house where Jesus was ministering and lowered him down to Jesus on a pallet. Doing so circumvented the crowd that stood between their friend and Jesus, who was their only hope (see Matthew 9:1-8; Mark 2:1-12; Luke 5:17-26). While the crowd saw the surprising action one way, Jesus saw it another. From His vantage point, He saw faith in Him that would be able to *accept* the forgiveness for sin that would be freely *given* to the whole world through Him.

> When Jesus saw their faith, he said to the paralytic, "Take heart, son; your sins are forgiven." (Matthew 9:2b)

The phrase *take heart* refers to a boldness that comes from inner assurance. It is what Joshua and the Israelites *received* from God before they *took* Canaan and what all men would be *given* opportunity to *receive* in Jesus. The assurance of personal salvation that would be *received* by faith in *accepting* Jesus as Christ/Messiah would embolden men to live beyond the natural by believing the supernatural of God. Some men, though, would find the seemingly illogical concept of salvation through forgiveness by faith in Jesus hard to believe.

> Now some teachers of the law were sitting there, thinking to themselves, "Why does this fellow talk like that? He's blaspheming! Who can forgive sins but God alone?" (Mark 2:5-7)

The teachers who were present had assessed the situation between Jesus and the paralytic correctly. Either Jesus had overstepped His limitations or He was God. But the conclusion to which the men's logic, based on limited knowledge, was leading them was incorrect. Their logic had ruled out the Truth, determining the actuality of Jesus being God to be impossibility. So, knowing the adjustment that those men and others needed in their thinking, Jesus *gave* them opportunity to witness the Truth that defied men's logic.

> [Jesus] said to them, "Why are you thinking these things? Which is easier to say to the paralytic, 'Your sins are forgiven,' or to say 'Get up, take your mat and walk'? But that you may know that the Son of Man has authority on earth to forgive sins" ... He said to the paralytic, "I tell you, get up, take your mat and go home." (Mark 2:8b-11)

*Get up... take your mat... go home.* These words were a bottom line synopsis by Jesus of why He was living among men. He was there to raise men up from death and *take* them Home to dwell permanently with God.

Mats were never intended to be full-time abodes, but portable resting places that provided men with some amount of comfort and cleanliness whenever they wanted to temporarily sit or lie down. Analogous to the tents that the Israelites had used in the wilderness, mats could be easily rolled up and transported, making their proper use beneficial.

But for the sick and the infirmed, who resided on them without reprieve, mats were indicative of restrictions that impeded their God-*given* freedom to come and go at will. As permanent dwelling places, both in and away from home, mats were more akin to prisons that offered no hope of release. But Jesus was present to expand men's lives, as well as their thinking. At His command, confinements ended, releasing men to live beyond the boundaries that sin had placed upon them. The need for men to "get up... and go home" was everywhere.

> [People] ran throughout that whole region and carried the sick on mats to wherever they heard [Jesus] was. And wherever he went---into villages, towns or countryside---they placed the sick in the marketplaces. They begged him to let them touch even the edge of his cloak, and all who touched him were healed. (Mark 6:55-56)

All who sought Jesus' help *received* it. He denied no one:

> Jesus went through all the towns and villages, teaching in their synagogues, preaching the good news of the kingdom and healing every disease and sickness. (Matthew 9:35)

Many followed him, and he healed all the sick (Matthew 12:15b; see also Matthew 4:24, 8:16, 14:14, 14:36, 15:30; Mark 6:56; Luke 4:40, 6:19; 9:11; Acts 10:38 for additional confirmation. Also, see Acts 5:16 with regard to Jesus healing all through the Apostles.)

But one day, at the Pool of Bethesda in Jerusalem, Jesus reached out to restore only one man, who did not even know who Jesus was, let alone what Jesus could do for him (see John 5:1-15). On that particular day, Jesus walked into a sea of invalids, who were positioned around the pool on their mats. They were all waiting for an angel to deliver a longshot miracle that would restore their lives to normal.

In that time and place, the belief was that when the pool's water was stirred by an angel (a messenger sent by God), then the first person to enter the water in its agitated state would be healed supernaturally. But the rarity of the agitation (supply) compared to the massive need for miracles (demand) created fierce competition among the invalids. With demand superseding supply, the pool area became an "every man for himself" territory that represented the condition of the world at large.

Entering the pool area, Jesus went over to an invalid who had been in need of *receiving* a miracle for thirty-eight long years to no avail. Then He asked a question of the man that sounded absurd.

> Do you want to get well?
> [Dost thou wish to become whole? —Young's Literal Translation (YLT)] (John 5:6b)

Far from absurd, the question served purpose. It *gave* the man opportunity to express the conclusion that he had reached after many years of personal, fruitless waiting. The man knew that his problem was not lack of desire, but lack of means. So he didn't use the question as a platform to regurgitate the details of the past, but as a springboard to future change by responding to Jesus' present tense question with ongoing need.

> "Sir," the man replied, "I have no one to help me ..."
> ["... Sir, I have no man ..." ---YLT] (John 5:7)

The invalid needed help to get beyond his natural situation and into supernatural resolution. But since the other invalids around the pool all had similar need and limitations, the man needed outside help---someone without similar restrictions.

Undoubtedly, during all of the man's long years of waiting, he had hoped, strategized and even prayed to the best of his ability to *receive* a miracle. Yet, in all of his time at the pool, he had never been in the right place at the right time to get one. By the time Jesus arrived, the man was not only well aware of his limitations, but he was also willing to publicly acknowledge them to Jesus. He needed a friend, not a competitor.

For nearly a millennia and a half, the Jewish people had been attempting and failing to live the Golden Rule: "Do to others as you would have them do to you" (Luke 6:31). God had specifically said to "love your neighbor as yourself" (Leviticus

19:18b), but they hadn't. Due to their sinful natures, they couldn't do so consistently without outside assistance: Jesus.

> Then Jesus said to [the invalid], "Get up! Pick up your mat and walk." At once the man was cured; he picked up his mat and walked. (John 5:8-9a)

That day at the pool, Jesus had appeared suddenly, remained only briefly and then slipped away. During His short visit, He had talked to only one man about his need. Then, after restoring that one man, Jesus had left. But He had also made a point of talking to the man again at the place of worship.

> Later Jesus met him at the temple and said to him, "See, you are well again. Stop sinning or something worse may happen to you." (John 5:14)

The events at the pool and Temple that day portrayed the bigger world event in which Jesus was fully engaged. Sent by God the Father, Jesus is the miracle of restorative salvation that all men need, but cannot attain on their own. Only Jesus, both willing and able, would be the Help needed by all men.

> For there is no difference between Jew and Gentile---the same Lord is Lord of all and richly blesses all who call on him, for, "Everyone who calls on the name of the Lord will be saved." (Romans 10:12-13)

But in the microcosmic world around the pool that day, Jesus did not restore everyone, but only one man. He did so with purpose, testifying in effect that He had been sent first to the Jews—one small nation that had been waiting for Him for a very long time. Salvation would first come to the Jews in the nation of Israel and then later to the Gentiles in all the world's nations.

Jesus' life as a man on the Earth lasted only a little over thirty-three years, and He ministered for a mere three and a half of those years. In that time, He walked among Jews, interacting with them and providing restoration, before leaving this world. The brevity of His stay was in man's best interest, for the sooner He departed, the sooner Holy Spirit would arrive. While Jesus, as a man, could only minister to one man at a time, Holy Spirit would minister simultaneously to unlimited number. The single healing at the pool *gave* men what was needed: opportunity to see the bigger picture of need of which they were all a part.

There came then another day in time when Jesus once again portrayed greater spiritual Truth while healing a specific individual (see John 9). This time, a question from the disciples prompted the lesson. Seeing a man born blind, they asked Jesus if the man's blindness was due to his sin or to the sin of his parents. Since the Jews were living under the Law, the question seemed logical to them. But its limiting assumptions revealed yet more of man's narrow-minded thinking. Jesus' response was an eye-opener in more ways than one.

> "Neither this man nor his parents sinned," said Jesus, "but this happened that the work of God might be displayed in his life." (John 9:3)

Mixing His saliva with some dirt, Jesus then made a mud that He smeared on the blind man's eyes. The mud's two components were of man and of the world. The physical concoction would have blinded anyone. But more important was the implication of spiritual blindness in men who cannot see through worldly concerns and their own physical nature to see the far greater spiritual realm of which they are a part.

When Jesus specifically sent the man to the Pool of Siloam (meaning *sent*) to wash away the mud, Jesus also sent a defining message. Jesus---the One sent by God---was the only way to remove the impediments to men's spiritual vision that would enable them to see the Truth of God's grace more clearly.

At the time when sin first entered man in the Garden of Eden, the focal point of man's vision shifted from the spiritual realm to the physical. The more he then continued focusing on himself, instead of on God, the more the scope of his vision narrowed. Though he still occasionally *received* rare peripheral glimpses of spiritual Truth, spiritual insight was *given* an overall backseat to physical dominance in men's general awareness. Jesus alone would be the means used by God to restore clarity to the understanding of Truth in men whose vision sin had muddied.

When the man returned from the Pool of Siloam, he was seeing for the very first time the world in which he had always lived. The event *gave* him new identity. Before his restoration, he had been just another man born blind. But afterward, he stood out from the crowd. As a man who had once been blind, but now could see (see

John 9:25), he had new stature, as well as a new outlook on the world, himself and God.

Jesus *took* every opportunity to maximize the potential of every moment of His brief ministry. Every one of His words and deeds served the Father's purpose of reconciling men to God for eternity. But in providing salvation for all mankind, Jesus never lost sight of the importance of any individual in this world or their specific needs. It mattered not whether a person was alone or in a crowd. To Jesus, each one stood out front and center.

Jesus called Matthew out of a tax collection booth (see Luke 5:27-32) and Zacchaeus out of a tree (see Luke 19:1-10). He went out of His way to lift the daughter of a synagogue ruler from her deathbed (see Mark 5:21-24, 35-43) and a Samaritan woman at a well from her life of shame (see John 4:1-42). He stopped for the woman who, isolated by a life-altering issue of blood, had dared to venture through crowds to get to Him (see Mark 5:24-34), as well as for a demoniac who, isolated by uncontrolled rage, was living like a wild animal among the dead in tombs (see Luke 8:26-39). He extended help to a child convulsing on the ground (see Mark 9:14-29) and to Peter's mother-in-law sick in a bed (see Mark 1:29-31).

Jesus sat with children (see Luke 18:15-17) and ate with sinners (see Matthew 9:10-13). He turned water to wine at a joyous wedding (see John 2:1-11) and stopped a widowed mother's tears at a funeral procession (see Luke 7:11-17). He multiplied food to relieve the hunger of the masses (see John 6:1-15) and nullified a storm to relieve the fear of His closest friends (see Mark 4:35-41). He revealed poverty in a rich young man (see Mark 10:17-23) and riches in a poor woman (see Mark 12:41-44). He broke the silence of deaf ears and mute voices (see Mark 7:31-37), freely enabling both the hearing and speaking of the Truth.

Jesus overlooked nothing. He lived every moment to its fullest harmonic accompaniment of each and every life that touched His, personally filling each specific need. Fully intimate with both God and man, Jesus joyfully served all, even when shedding tears (see John 11:1-37; Luke 19:41-44; Hebrews 5:7).

Thousands of people affected by the services that Jesus rendered followed His every move and came to know Him to varying degrees. Seventy-two knew Him well enough to be sent out as His hands and feet, healing people and proclaiming the coming kingdom (see Luke 10:1-20). Twelve knew Him well enough to commune with Him at the Last Supper. Three knew Him well enough to witness the transfiguration (see Mark 9:2-13). But on the Cross, Jesus would be alone. Until Jesus would pave the way through death, no man could follow Him. He had to go first. He had to go where they could not (see John 13:36).

From the disciples' point of view, the time of Jesus' death arrived much too quickly. They wanted more time with the Man who they had come to love. But He wanted eternity with them—those whom He had always loved. So Jesus went to the Cross the same way that He lived: in loving service to others.

Without question, Jesus was crucified. That is certain. Historical records apart from the Bible confirm so. On the Cross,

Jesus died. Of that, medical experts are assured by John's testimony. John saw the blood and water that flowed from Jesus' side when a soldier pierced Jesus' body with a spear while Jesus was still on the Cross (see John 19:34). Dead, the body of Jesus was buried---deposited in a tomb that was sealed and guarded by Roman soldiers under Pilate's orders (see Matthew 27:62-66).

Jesus' life in mortal flesh was finished. As He had *given* up heavenly life to come to the Earth, He *gave* up earthly life to *take* men to heaven by way of a three part baptism: blood, water and Spirit. Each baptism testifies to Truth, and together they unify as a three part delivery of the whole of salvation's totality: death, burial and life everlasting.

> For there are three that testify: the Spirit, the water and the blood; and the three are in agreement. (1 John 5:7-8)
> We were therefore buried with him through baptism into death in order that, just as Christ was raised from the dead through the glory of the Father, we too may live a new life. (Romans 6:4)

The timeless Cross of Jesus can be seen from two perspectives: men's and God's. While the Cross is an instrument of death employed by sinful men who acted unjustly, doing evil, it is more so an instrument of life employed by a righteous God who carried out justice, doing good. While men look at the Cross and see the horror of brutal suffering, God looks at the Cross and sees suffering's end.

The more men get to know Jesus, the more clearly they see the love of God. The more love they see, the more their faith in God is strengthened---settled, established, firmed up. The more their faith is strengthened, the more peace they experience. In peace with God, wholeness occurs. Life is renewed---restored to complete soundness---by faith in Christ Jesus (see Acts 3:16).

Wholeness is the work that God accomplished in Christ Jesus on the Cross. Wholeness of body, soul and spirit... Wholeness of Family relationship... Wholeness of Creation... All have been accomplished by a whole God---Father, Son and Holy Spirit. Nothing is missing except for the unwinding of the last of time, which once having been set in motion by God continues ticking, fulfilling its good purpose. One day, it too will be perfectly complete in bringing the events of Christ's return.

In the end, God's perfection will be seen in His full glory that is revealed to men from within the spiritual realm in which they have always lived. Nothing will be hidden. Truth, clearly visible, will be seen by all: Jesus *is* reality (see Colossians 2:17).

> There is one body and one Spirit---just as you were called to one hope when you were called---one Lord, one faith, one baptism; one God and Father of all, who is over all, through all and in all. (Ephesians 4:4-6)

Once men are saved and "... hidden with Christ in God" (Colossians 3:3), they are "... dead to sin, but alive to God" (Romans 6:11). They are sanctified, made holy unto God (see 1 Corinthians

1:2), reconciled to God, made One with Him forever (see 2 Corinthians 5:19). In eternity, far beyond men's present scope of comprehension, there exists only more of God's completeness for men to continually come to know.

Far more than making whole, *God is Wholeness...* beginning to end, period.

# *The Conferring* (Holy Spirit)

When Jesus called men to discipleship, saying "Come, follow me" (Matthew 4:19a; see also John 1:39, 1:43), He called them to do far more than tag along. He called them to walk into transformed lives, transforming the world.

The adventure of following Jesus would be one of unimaginable proportion, enabling men to realize and *receive* the Father's heart through personal relationship with the Son. Drawn by and to the Father's loving-goodness in Jesus, men would become God's manifested good will on Earth. Into the world they would go, doing God's good work among men by sharing the Good News of salvation with others. Extending invitations to others to join them in *receiving* Jesus as personal Savior, they would further extend the knowledge of God's loving-goodness throughout the world to one soul after another.

But each person so introduced to Jesus would have to choose their own personal level of engagement with Him. Jesus never limits intimacy with anyone, but wants to be fully known, just as each man is fully known by Jesus (see 1 Corinthians 13:12). For in those personal relationships with Jesus, the Father is building fellowship between men and Him (see 1 Corinthians 1:9).

Each man who hears of Jesus is free to enter into one of four relationship categories with Him. He can turn his back on Jesus and walk away, refusing an introduction. He can meet Jesus, but never personally get to know Him. He can spend time with Jesus, studying Him, but refrain from *giving* Jesus complete reign over him. Or he can get as close as possible to Jesus, submitting himself to Jesus' complete and personal care.

To Jesus' dismay, there were many men in His day who scoffed at Him and went their own way, leading others astray. Religious men, who chose to capitalize on personal investment in regulations instead of enjoying the freedom *given* in intimacy with Jesus, missed the opportunity of a lifetime to befriend God by befriending Jesus. One day, in the best interest of all, Jesus made a point of pointing out the error in their thinking.

> And he said to them: "You have a fine way of setting aside the commands of God in order to observe your own traditions." (Mark 7:9)

These men, who incorrectly presumed that their security rested in self-righteous works, were set in their ways. Other individuals were willing to follow Jesus, but only to self-defined boundaries. Refusing to leave their personal comfort zones, these men were guilty of over-intellectualizing their relationships with Jesus. They depended more on personal comprehension than they did on faith in Jesus. When Jesus called Himself "the bread of life" (John 6:35) of which men would eat, many of His followers decided that they had heard enough, and they refused to follow Him any farther (see John 6:52-66). By closing their minds, choosing not to *receive* further instruction from Jesus, their misinterpretation of His words became home-made barriers that hindered the right fellowship with God that Jesus was building.

> On hearing it, many of his disciples said, "This is a hard teaching. Who can accept it?" (John 6:60)

> From this time many of his disciples turned back and no longer followed him. (John 6:66)

But then there were those who chose to go all the way with Jesus, *accepting* even death in His Name. These men knew that they had no other name on which they could depend.

> "You do not want to leave, too, do you?" Jesus asked the Twelve. (John 6:67)

> Simon Peter answered him, "Lord, to whom shall we go? You have the words of eternal life. We believe and know that you are the Holy One of God." (John 6:69)

In the end, Jesus' true disciples would, in fact, never leave Him. But the time had to come when Jesus was going to have to leave them for a while. He said so specifically after the Last Supper, also telling them about the coming Holy Spirit.

> I tell you the truth, anyone who has faith in me will do what I have been doing. He will do even greater things than these, because I am going to the Father. (John 14:12)

> And I will ask the Father, and he will give you another Counselor to be with you forever---the Spirit of truth. The world cannot accept him, because it neither sees him nor

knows him. But you know him for he lives with you and will be in you. I will not leave you as orphans. I will come to you. (John 14:16-18)

But the Counselor, the Holy Spirit, whom the Father will send you in my name will teach you all things and will remind you of everything I have said to you. (John 14:12, 16-18, 26)

Holy Spirit (God!) was coming to the Earth to *take* residence in men! God Himself would be men's Enabler, empowering them with Truth that would change the world. The strengthening of God's Kingdom would occur from within Spirit filled men, who would otherwise remain limited without Him. Jesus instructed His disciples to wait for the Holy Spirit.

Do not leave Jerusalem, but wait for the gift my Father promised, which you have heard me speak about. For John baptized with water, but in a few days you will be baptized by the Holy Spirit. (Acts 1:4b-5)

So the disciples waited until the Holy Spirit descended from above and entered into them on Pentecost---the celebration of the Law's arrival through Moses at Mt. Sinai, fifty days after the first Sabbath following Passover (see Leviticus 23). On that day, Holy Spirit birthed the universal Church in one hundred twenty individuals, who had each chosen to entrust their eternal souls to Jesus, the risen Savior (see Acts 1:12-15, 2:1).

Suddenly a sound like the blowing of a violent wind came from heaven and filled the whole house where they were sitting. They saw what seemed to be tongues of fire that separated and came to rest on each of them. All of them were filled with the Holy Spirit and began to speak in other tongues as the Spirit enabled them. (Acts 2:2-4)

With Holy Spirit residing in them, the first Christians walked boldly out into a hurting world that needed Jesus. Not only did they walk with God, as others had done previously, but with God *in* them, empowering them to live the Truth, God's way. They all shared one common job description *given* by Jesus.

Therefore go and make disciples of all nations, baptizing them in the name of the Father, of the Son and of the Holy Spirit, and teaching them to obey everything I have commanded you. (Matthew 28:19a)

As you go, preach this message: The kingdom of heaven is near. Heal the sick, raise the dead, cleanse those who have leprosy, drive out demons. Freely you have received, freely give. (Matthew 10:7-8)

Only after men's hearts would be transformed by God in salvation would men be able to truly *give* as needed in the Name of Jesus. Those choosing to *receive* neither salvation in Christ nor accompanying Holy Spirit empowerment would continue having only fleeting satisfaction to offer anyone. Jesus asserted that lasting Kingdom good would come only through the King.

Not everyone who says to me "Lord, Lord" will enter the kingdom of heaven, but only he who does the will of my Father who is in heaven. Many will say to me on that day, "Lord, Lord, did we not prophesy in your name, and in your name drive out demons and perform many miracles?"

Then I will tell them plainly, "I never knew you. Away from me, you evil-doers!" (Matthew 7:21-23)

The depth of each man's relationship with Jesus would be a major factor in determining personal *acceptance* or not of the reality of God's Holy Spirit Presence in this world. Jesus' life was not based on performance standards that He strove to achieve, and neither does God desire for any man's life to be so defined. Rather, Jesus lived in connection to the Father by Holy Spirit empowerment from within. As the Father *gave* Holy Spirit publicly to the Son for man's sake, so are all men to also *receive* Him after confessing faith in Jesus. Living without Holy Spirit's indwelling Presence versus with Him is as different as night is to day.

Night and day---darkness and light---respectively represent life without God (Father, Son and Holy Spirit) and life with the Three-in-One. While the first fosters ignorance and sin, the second disperses Truth and righteousness.

After Holy Spirit descended supernaturally from above on Pentecost and entered into the individuals who awaited Him, those same individuals carried Holy Spirit out the door in their physical bodies in God's Self-distribution plan. God multiplies His Presence in this world through Holy Spirit Presence in men. Every time another individual *receives* Spirit baptism, the light of Jesus' eternal life shines brighter to extend hope further.

The hope that God had *given* to mankind in the promise of a son---a son who was to be *given* to Abraham, the father of the faith---was not fleeting, but transcendent---of God and above all worldly trials. The promise pointed to Jesus and the light of hope that Jesus would spark in a very dark world, enabling all to see the Truth of God's grace in God's own light (see John 1:4-9).

> I am the light of the world. Whoever follows me, will never walk in darkness, but will have the light of life. (John 8:12b)

After Saul (Paul) of Tarsus was blinded by the light of Jesus on the road to Damascus, God restored Saul through the disciple Ananias. By Ananias placing his hands on Saul, Ananias served God and men, leading Saul into salvation. Saul's restoration through Ananias by Holy Spirit power began Paul's new life of ministry. Through Saul's conversion, the discipleship of Ananias would disciple multitudes. Hope's light would spread in a dark world by God's Spirit Presence within these two men to ignite uncountable others to *receive* life-everlasting in Jesus.

> Placing his hands on Saul, [Ananias] said, "Brother Saul, the Lord---Jesus, who appeared to you on the road as you were coming here, has sent me so that you may see again and be filled with the Holy Spirit. (Acts 9:17b)

Once Paul had *received* salvation and Holy Spirit power, he could not do less than share the Gospel. He explained why.

> I am compelled to preach. (1 Corinthians 9:16)

> For Christ's love compels us, because we are convinced that one died for all, and therefore all died. And he died for all, that those who live should no longer live for themselves but

for him who died for them and raised again. (2 Corinthians 5:14-15)

Having *received* everlasting hope from God, Paul, as a Christian, then had hope to *give*. So Paul *gave*, as he had been *given*: freely. The delay seen in Jesus' return is actually in men's best interest, for it is *giving* Christians opportunity to spread more light, *giving* hope to other souls who are still in darkness.

> But do not forget this one thing, dear friends: With the Lord a day is like a thousand years, and a thousand years are like a day. The Lord is not slow in keeping his promise, as some understand slowness. He is patient with you, not wanting anyone to perish, but everyone to come to repentance. (2 Peter 3:8-9; see also Psalm 90:4)

Far more than hopeful, *God is Hope...* beginning to end, period.

# *The Knowing* (The Eternal Word)

**W**ith divine knowledge and wisdom filling His every word, God speaks life-filled hope into every situation. His words provide men with knowledge that produces closer intimacy with Him, enabling a deeper abiding: continuing, dwelling, staying, remaining.

The Word of God is purifying. It strains error from men's thinking, clarifying understanding. The Word of God is powerful, doing God's will, distributing His loving-goodness throughout Creation. The Word of God is present, making all things right.

> How can a young man keep his way pure? By living according to your word. ... Your word is a lamp to my feet and a light for my path. ... The unfolding of your words gives light; it gives understanding to the simple. (Psalm 119:9, 105, 130)

> For with you is the fountain of life; in your light we see light. (Psalm 36:9)

When God *gave* Adam and Cain specific instructions regarding their actions, He did so clearly and simply for their benefit. His words left no room for ambiguity. Each man was *given* the information that was in his best interest to *receive*. Yet neither man chose to live according to God's words, but rather disregarded them. Doing so equated to rejecting God, for God and His words are inseparable. As God is, so is His Word.

> As for God, his way is perfect; the word of the LORD is flawless. (Psalm 18:30a)

> God is not a man that he should lie, nor a son of man that he should change his mind. Does he speak and then not act? Does he promise and not fulfill? (Numbers 23:19)

God's words define His Being to men who cannot see Him. His words are connectors, conveying godly knowledge and wisdom to men, building faith in God, promoting peace. God's words do good, undoing evil through their divine rightness.

> My son, do not forget my teaching, but keep my commands in your heart, for they will prolong your life many years and bring you prosperity. (Proverbs 3:1-2)

> Do not be wise in your own eyes; fear the LORD and shun evil. (Proverbs 2:7)

> Blessed is the man who finds wisdom, who gains understanding, for she is more profitable than silver and yields better returns than gold. (Proverbs 3:13-14)

> The fear of the LORD is the beginning of wisdom, and knowledge of the Holy One is understanding. (Proverbs 9:10)

> For the LORD gives wisdom, and from his heart come knowledge and understanding. (Proverbs 2:6)

Words emanating from God, who is light (see 1 John 1:5b), are utilized by Him in the promotion of life's perfection. Eliminating sin's darkness, God's correction of men's wrong thinking is a gift of loving-goodness that is *given* from Father God to His beloved children in the unending best interest of all.

> My son, do not despise the LORD's discipline and do not resent his rebuke, because the LORD disciplines those he loves, as a father the son he delights in. (Proverbs 3:11-12; see also Hebrews 12:5-11)
>
> Do not my words do good to him whose ways are upright? (Micah 2:7b)
>
> Hold onto instruction, do not let it go; guard it well, for it is your life. (Proverbs 4:13)

The totality of life is not as men most often think it to be. In eternal reality, life has no ticking clock, no night, no frenzy, no sweat, no pain, no tears, no shortfalls, no ending---nothing to hamper uninterrupted satisfaction. It is limitless, without bounds, forever becoming greater than it currently is. It is endless freedom in endless existence to experience endless perfection. It provides endless insight into endless knowledge, endlessly fulfilling men's desire for more. It contains no emptiness, no voids, but is always full of itself.

The restrictions of this world that cloak eternity, keeping it hidden from physical view, serve divine purpose. They are instrumental in preparing men to *receive* maximum benefit from co-existing everlastingly with God---the Spirit Source of all life. The world is not a stage of performers, who must measure up to unattainable God-sized standards to enter into God's Presence. But rather, it is a preparation ground---a learning center, where everlasting gratefulness for existence is developed and where appreciation for every aspect of life matures. It is where men learn under God's tutelage to rest in His good and loving grace, thereby enabling men to freely care for all others more than self.

This world, a divinely designed laboratory of sorts, *gives* men opportunity to gain hands-on experiential knowledge of what matters in life and what doesn't. It is where conflicts are worked out to obtain peace within, through ongoing acquisition of Truth. It is where opportunity for trial and error leads to greater discernment of good and evil, heightening awareness of the goodness of God. It is where men learn that *giving* and *receiving* are wrapped up together as one. It is where men are *given* opportunity to grow by faith in God in ways that exceed their natural ability to do so, resulting in everlasting praise and thanksgiving being offered to God in right worship of Him.

When God first instructed Moses to lead the Israelites out of bondage, Moses, in essence, wanted proof that he could do so simply because God had said so. Moses knew his own limitations fairly well, but as of then he had little previous personal experience with God that he could bank upon. Therefore Moses wanted God to somehow assure the words that He had *given* to Moses. Instead, God *gave* Moses an explanation of the proper working order within their relationship, letting Moses know that there was only one path forward to Moses *receiving* such assurance of God.

> And God said, "I will be with you. And this will be the sign to you that it is I who have sent you. When you have

brought the people out of Egypt, you will worship me on this mountain." (Exodus 3:12)

Only after Moses had completed the *given* task in faith, and he had experienced the seemingly impossible in accordance with God's words, would the experience itself become the proof that Moses wanted upfront. The journey would be made by faith in God's *given* Word or it wouldn't occur. Only by *taking* God at His Word throughout the journey would Moses gain trusting knowledge of God that would lead him to truly worship God.

The same is true for all men. Only by stepping out in faith in agreement with God's Word, staking life upon it to one degree or another, can men see the miraculous unfold, delivering benefit. To personally know the Truth of God in this world requires men to "taste and see that the LORD is good" (Psalm 34:8a). Only the faith of tasting produces desired affirmation. Inaction from a lack of faith that fails to produce desired results, thereby only enhancing further doubt of God's Word, does in itself circuitously support the fact that God's Word is indeed always integrally interwoven with faith.

> From the fruit of his mouth a man's stomach is filled; with the harvest from his lips he is satisfied. The tongue has the power of life and death, and those who love it will eat its fruit. (Proverbs 18:20-21)

God forces no man to choose right over wrong, good over evil, knowledge over ignorance. Instead, in man's best interest, God, true to His Word, allows each man to freely choose life or death for himself. From the beginning, God has *given* man the autonomy he desires to do as he pleases. Man has always been free to come to God or to go his own way. Laying all of the cards on the table, so to speak, God has presented Truth clearly, *giving* each man opportunity to see and believe the Truth for himself.

Only when a man *accepts* God's Word in this world, does eternal life become his current reality, *giving* completeness to the intended good for which God's Word has been *given*. God's Word is for here and now, which, though but a smidgen of eternity, contains the doorway through which men must pass to enter eternal life. The only way to do so is to *receive* the Word of the Living God personally, to *receive* Jesus as life-*giving* Truth.

> I am the Living One; I was dead, and behold I am alive for ever and ever! And I hold the keys of death and Hades. (Revelation 1:18)

> Here I am! I stand at the door and knock. If anyone hears my voice and opens the door, I will come in and eat with him, and he with me. (Revelation 3:20)

Faith in Jesus is the key to entering eternal life. Jesus supernaturally manifests God's powerful Spirit-Word Presence in this world through men's faith in His Name. Personal knowledge of Jesus that is *received* by God's grace opens men's hearts to *receive* the love of God for them in ever-increasing magnitude. All who invite Jesus into their hearts feed on His abundant life in Family communion at the Father's Table.

And [Jesus] took bread, gave thanks and broke it, and gave it to them, saying, "This is my body given for you; do this in remembrance of me."

And in the same way, after the supper, he took the cup, saying, "This is the new covenant in my blood, which is poured out for you." (Luke 22:19-20)

Family communion has existed eternally between Father, Son and Holy Spirit. Into that singular eternity a new dimension of time was drawn from the Family's communion in order that the communion might feed others beyond itself. Into time, the Three-in-One Godhead birthed a man, who was *given* a breath of life in order to get the man's life started (see Genesis 2:7)

The man was *given* all good things, so that he, too, might flourish in Family goodness and decide to join in the Family meal. But instead, he chose to eat from a table that he built for himself, only to realize later that no matter how much he ate, he was always hungry for more (see Ecclesiastes 6:7). Nothing to which he put his hands was able to satisfy him for very long.

The God who had created man watched him intently and continued to offer to provide him with all that he needed for a full life. But the offers were repeatedly rejected due to the man's lack of knowledge of what he was declining.

So, in agreement, the Three-in-One chose to do what was best. They chose to suffer incomprehensible separation to keep the man from dying in isolation. For his sake, they did what needed to be done. The Father sent the Son to feed the man all the Truth that He had to offer.

> The Word became flesh and made his dwelling among us. We have seen his glory, the glory of the One and Only, who came from the Father, full of grace and truth. (John 1:14)

> He was in the world, and though the world was made through him, the world did not recognize him. He came to that which was his own, but his own did not receive him. Yet, to those who received him, to those who believed in his name, he gave the right to become children of God— (John 1:10-12)

The Son *gave* His all to satisfy the man's hunger. He filled the man with His own abundant life of grace and Truth.

> [M]an does not live on bread alone, but on every word that comes from the mouth of the LORD. (Deuteronomy 8:3b)

The Family of Three held nothing back in filling the man's need. In order for the Son to *give* His all to the man, the Father disconnected from the Son, leaving the Son to go into the man's dark isolation and bring him out. Cut off from His Family, the Son suffered, and so did the Family during the separation. But during that time, their eternal love spilled out upon the man from all Three to fill the man's emptiness with the life in the Son's freely *given* blood.

> This is how God showed his love among us: He sent his one and only Son into the world that we might live through him. This is love: not that we loved God, but that he loved

us and sent his Son as an atoning sacrifice for our sins. (1 John 4:9, 10)

The Son *took* the man's death upon Himself, and the man lived. So did the Son, whose sacrifice *gave* life. The Family rejoiced in uninterrupted unity that remained forever constant.

Who shall separate us from the love of Christ? (Romans 8:35a)

[N]either death nor life, neither angels nor demons, neither the present nor the future, nor any powers, neither height nor depth, nor anything else in all creation, will be able to separate us from the love of God that is in Christ Jesus our Lord. (Romans 8:38-39)

In gratitude, the man *gave* his life to the Son who had saved him, and the two became One. In the Son, the man also became One with the Father and the Spirit, and the Family grew. God the Three-in-One was pleased to no end, literally, for He knew that the Oneness of the Family's eternal bond would only gain strength in expanded unification through the Son, forever *giving* increasing glory to all that is good and right.

Independent of gender, nationality or religious background, each person fills a specially designated position in God's time continuum. Each one is *given* a unique time, place and way to *receive* the love of God for them that was revealed to the world in Christ Jesus. That love is never secret, but eternally demonstrative, glorifying God above and before all.

The LORD appeared to us in the past, saying: "I have loved you with an everlasting love; I have drawn you with loving kindness. I will build you up again and you will be rebuilt ..." (Jeremiah 31:3-4a)

In *giving* all, God *received* the Family that He wanted, the Family that would fill His desire to *give* His loving-goodness evermore with ever-increasing abundant joy. Unencumbered by sin, His Family would continue *receiving* Him in overflowing capacity, becoming fountains of His good love by grace through faith, endlessly magnifying God forever.

Whoever is wise, let him heed these things and consider the great love of the LORD. (Psalm 107:43)

This is love's epicenter: love freely *gives* all. The Father did, *giving* His Son, and so did the Son, *giving* His life.

Far more than loving, *"God is love"* (1 John 4:8, 16), always... without beginning... without end... and no period... ever...

# CONCLUDING WORDS: Your Story

Before time existed, you were a desire of God. God desired you! The exact time and place of your creation were planned before the Earth was formed. Your birth was not haphazard, nor accidental. It was divinely executed. You were a wanted child, whose every detail was thoughtfully and lovingly designed to create your uniqueness---your specialness to God Almighty. You are one-of-a-kind and no one could ever take your place in the mind and heart of God, for He made you to be an irreplaceable receptacle of His everlasting loving-goodness.

So loved by God were you in your spiritual conception within Him that He created a physical world into which He could birth you specifically. He *gave* you a world that would provide you with the greatest benefit from the life that He chose to breathe into you, *giving* you the same choice to love and be loved as God Himself had made in creating you for that very purpose.

In God, choice and love are integrally interwoven. They cannot be separated one from the other for they are mutually inclusive in their emanation from God. In His sovereignty, God has total freedom to do as He pleases, and His pleasure is in choosing to love you in ever greater measure. That decision is made in full awareness that *giving* love includes the possibility of love's rejection. Yet, because of love's divine nature in God, love is not thwarted by the possibility, but strengthened in its decision to freely *give* itself away, even in the midst of being misunderstood and/or under appreciated. Thereby, love flourishes in patient endurance that knows only joy in its unyielding refusal to be either self-serving or deterred from its own good purpose.

True love, coming from God alone, knows only unparalleled goodness. It has the power to negate any personal price associated in this world with its unequivocal distribution, overcoming lack of *acceptance* with greater self-sacrifice. Even in the face of opposition, love simply expands itself more by continuing to freely *give* itself away. It can be neither hindered from its *giving* nor coerced into *giving*, for love sets no limitation on personal expenditure nor any expectation of personal return on its investment. Rather, it *gives* for the sole pleasure of seeing love's benefits increasingly abound in all.

So from within God's eternal love, God designed a place in time's continuum that only you can fill. Explicitly, He positioned you where His good purpose in your life is best fulfilled in your *acceptance* of His love for you and all of His Creation. Your existence in this world is in the place and time that best benefits your life and the lives of others that divinely overlap yours. You are not a fluke of nature or the result of man's whim, but a work of art from the heart of God---a work that is perfected in your *acceptance* of His love for all. In you, God's love creates a piece of heaven on Earth, where you are God's likeness, just the way God always planned for you to be.

But before God created either the world or you, He also knew of your every sinful shortcoming and your overwhelming need to be fully loved in the midst of shame and regret. In that knowledge, He chose by love's divine wisdom to breathe His life into you and *give* you opportunity to know love's perfection.

God loved you personally through every moment of time. He thought of you in the coming and going of each man's life on Earth, especially that of His beloved Son in whom His love for you was most fully revealed. In God's personal sacrifice of His One and Only Son for your sake, God's unprecedented *giving* declared unprecedented love for you to all Creation. By pouring out Jesus's life-*giving* blood, God made provision for you---an empty vessel----to be filled with His love and, therefore, with His Being, who arrived in the Person of the Holy Spirit. In the union of God's sacrificial *giving* and your confessed need, God created perfect everlasting relationship between you and Him, expanding love's limitless perfection that is always freely *given.*

With perfect love---God Himself---alive in you, you *receive* enablement to *give* as God *gives*:  immeasurably and steadfastly, without exception. The love and the choice are yours. God made it so from the beginning. In light of God's love, it could be no other way. So, as it turns out, even if you remain an unanswered question, God never is. He is the same, always loving all ways.

# A FINAL WORD: A Personal Story

There was no contest. Jesus simply won. His hands-down victory came by way of Jesus holding His hands out to His sides, as He offered Himself for sacrifice. In effect, those hands said, "Go ahead. Pin me down. Find out what I'm made of. Take your best shot."

So sin did. Nails went in, and the Cross went up. The hands of Jesus, free to point an accusatory finger at all men, instead pointed to Jesus' reason for hanging between two sinners, one contrite and the other one not. Jesus was the demarcation line between the repentant and the arrogant, the humble and the proud, the living and the dead. The hands that had touched a leper, blessed children and broken bread now touched hearts in a new way, blessing each person who would be broken by the love of God for them in Jesus.

I was there when Jesus was crucified, at least in spirit, if not in body. I had been hanging out with Jesus for quite some time, watching His every move and listening to His every word. I had celebrated with Him at the wedding feast in Cana and wept with Him at the tomb of Lazarus. I had traversed dusty roads, following Him around the Galilean countryside and back-and-forth to and from Jerusalem. I had seen lepers be cleansed, the paralyzed walk, the hungry fed and the sea stilled. But I had never expected to see what I saw upon the Cross: Jesus loving me to His death. His heart and hands bled for *me*. He drew me to Him by the pouring out of Himself for my sake.

The knowledge that Jesus loved me had been with me since childhood Sunday school days. But as an adult living in awareness of personal imperfection among a world full of others in need, Jesus' death for all mankind was much easier to fully accept than was His death for me specifically. The reality of that kind of sacrificial love for me couldn't quite penetrate a shield of doubt that kept the seemingly unlikely at bay.

For years, regrets and disappointments had stacked up like stones to form a wall---a hedge of self-protection---around my hurting heart. But the wall that had seemed so necessary and so right for so long was revealed from Jesus' vantage point to be anything but protective. It was debilitating and self-defeating.

So fortified was the wall that, for a long time, I feared the ridiculous: not even Jesus would be able to fully disarm its automatic defense mechanism. But day and night, Jesus fought the battle to win my heart. He spoke of my importance to Him in uncountable ways. His every word of Truth disclosed more of God's loving-goodness for me, creating an opening for intimacy that weakened the wall.

Tenaciously, Jesus' nail-scarred hands lifted stone after stone, casting them all aside. In time, the wall came down, dismantled by love. Any one of those stones could have been used to stone---condemn---me, for each stone bore witness to self-centered concern.

But Jesus didn't do that. Instead, He freed my heart to receive life abundant. Through His nail holes, He handed me a life of grace.

As the wall had diminished, pretense had also declined, for Truth prevailed in restoring wholeness. The Truth is that each life matters to God greatly, so much so that Jesus was born into a condemned world and the Holy Spirit descended and remained in a resurrected one. God's love is never distant or generic, but is always up-close and personal.

As I looked to the Cross of Jesus for understanding, my limited concept of reality metamorphosed into comprehension of greater Truth. Jesus extended my vision by transforming my thinking. He enabled me to better accept God's heart, openly displayed in Him, as He endured rejection in the giving of acceptance that promoted others' welfare.

Jesus is love's hallmark, its fullness. That is why Jesus couldn't lose and why there was no contest. Perfect love, fully applied, couldn't fail, but only perfect. While people can fail to love, love never fails people... ever.

Jesus didn't fail me.

He won't fail you.

--------------------------------

*"Give thanks to the LORD, for he is good;*
*his love endures forever."*
(Psalm 118:1, 29—both the beginning and the end)

# References Cited

Strong, James. *Strong's Exhaustive Concordance of the Bible: Updated Edition.* Peabody, MA: Hendrickson Publishers, 2007.

Zondervan. BibleGateway. www.biblegateway.com. 2016

\*\*\*\*\*\*\*\*

Other writings by Cathy Scott

can be read or located via

www.ThisIsWhatHappened.net

\*\*\*\*\*\*\*\*

Cover Design: While the author sat in her living room typing *The Life of the* Cross, the first of *The Cross* series of books, a dense fog obscured the sixty mile view from the living room windows of the mountain home. At one point, the author looked up to discover that the fog had completely lifted and that three small clouds had taken its place. A short vertical cloud and a short horizontal cloud formed a perfect cross in the middle of the field of vision, and a third small, puffy cloud, just above the upper left quadrant of the cross, was immediately recognized by the author as a crown. The Cross and the Crown...